canning cents

the money-saving whole foods canning handbook

Front Table Books
An imprint of Cedar Fort, Inc.
Springville, Utah

Stephanie
Petersen

ISBN 13: 978-1-4621-1523-5

Published by Front Table Books, an imprint of Cedar Fort, Inc.
2373 W. 700 S., Springville, UT 84663
Distributed by Cedar Fort, Inc., www.cedarfort.com

LIBRARY OF CONGRESS CATALOGING-IN-PUBLICATION DATA

Petersen, Stephanie.
Canning cents / Stephanie Petersen.
  pages cm
Includes bibliographical references and index.
ISBN 978-1-4621-1523-5
1. Canning and preserving. I. Title.

TX603.P48 2015
641.4'2--dc23

2014037234

Cover design by Bekah Claussen
Cover design © 2015 Lyle Mortimer
Edited by Justin Greer

Printed in the United States of America

10 9 8 7 6 5 4 3 2 1

contents

foreword

Welcome to eating healthy whole foods on a shoestring. As a chef and a mom, I have been ever conscious of the changes in the food industry over the last few decades. As a friend to farmers and home gardeners, I know what it takes to bring fresh produce to the table. I have seen the rising cost of fresh foods. I understand how hard it is to feed a busy family. I have struggled with a tight food budget for many years and heard on many different fronts that it was almost impossible to eat healthy whole foods on a low budget. When I left the traditional restaurant scene and became a full-time mother, a large part of my new life was saving money on our family's food budget so that I could be home. This meant that I made everything from scratch and watched every penny. I know I am not the first mother who ever had to watch the budget closely. I did what needed to be done. I trust you are doing the best you can as well. I found, for the most part, that many of my friends and family were spending a great deal more on their food than I was—and we were eating whole foods. Now, as a full-time working mother, we still do it. Though a few things have changed with teenage boys, and though my food budget has gone up a lot over the last couple of years, one thing that hasn't changed is my passion for saving money and eating well. One of the best ways to do this is to home preserve.

introduction

my beginnings

I grew up in a home with a kitchen pantry that was always well stocked with home-canned products. My father is a Master Gardener, and we always had a large garden that filled the entire yard. My dad is still known for his remarkable green thumb. There was always bounty from the glorious garden to be put in jars and processed for feeding the family all year long. My mother is a masterful home chef with a degree in home economics education and food science. Imagine growing up in a home with parents like that, and you can understand what makes me so passionate about real food. Know too that we were not at all what most people would call wealthy. It was a humble life. When I close my eyes and think about those years, there are two things that carried us through: love and hard work.

beginnings for you

If you are new to home canning and preserving, I am writing this book for you. I hope to share some of my keys for success in not only saving money but preserving food, keys that can make a big impact on your health and the health of those you love. In this book, I will be sharing my most cherished recipes from years of canning with my family. I will be sharing my insights and my struggles. I will be cheering you onward to success. I will be sharing my heart. It is my sincere hope that this book will empower you to take a firm hold on your family's food budget and move forward confidently. Working together elbow to elbow and heart to heart is powerful. Consider me your new best friend in the kitchen. Grab your mason jars and embrace your pioneering spirit. We're going on a canning adventure! Onward and upward!

chapter one

home canning basics

canning principles

Home canning is taking your food one step beyond just cooking. It is preventing food from spoiling or naturally deteriorating. It is important to do this safely, and there are some basic principles that will empower you to do so. I am not going to introduce any new canning techniques in this book. I am a chef, not a food scientist. What I am going to be sharing with you are the methods that are scientifically proven (and from reputable sources) to prevent the growth of potentially lethal organisms in your food. I don't want to scare anyone. On the contrary, I want to make you aware of what you need to know when home canning to protect your family. The principles of canning are designed to create an ideal condition for optimum freshness, with the least possible opportunity for the growth of molds, yeasts, spores, and bacteria. These are the principles you need to master.

conditions for success

Everything in life needs the right condition for success. If you want a garden to grow, you give your soil the proper treatments. If you don't want weeds to flourish, you take necessary precautions. If you want children to be successful, you give them all the right conditions at home and school to do their best. By the same token, if you want germs, molds, and yeast to grow, give them something warm, moist, and full of food. The environment in a canning jar has the potential to be the best condition ever for the growth of horrible stuff. When you control the conditions in your home-canned products so that they are the least appealing place for microorganisms to grow, you will have your best success.

heat processing

Canning interrupts the natural decay and spoilage of food products by heating the food in a home canning jar, tightly closed, in a vacuum environment. Heat applied and held for the proper amount of time ensures that potential microorganisms are killed. That same heat that destroys the organisms helps create a vacuum seal, preventing other organisms from having access to food in the jar. This seal is created during cooling when the lid seals to the jar. This practice is called *processing*. It is a method of proper temperature processing that must be employed, along with the proper amount of time exposed to the heat, to destroy normal levels of heat-resistant microorganisms. I will refer often to "processing times" in this book. This is the most pivotal step in canning.

some frequently asked questions about home canning

What are the requirements for safe home canning?
Heat and acid level are the two keys to canning safety. High-acid foods such as plums and rhubarb are quite resistant to bacteria and only require the "boiling water-bath" method of canning. Low-acid foods—including most vegetables, meats, and seafood—must be canned at higher temperatures, temperatures that only a pressure canner can attain. We will be exploring both of these canning methods in this book.

What jars are best for canning?

Manufacturers make heavy-duty jars specifically for home canning. Do not use, say, empty peanut butter jars, because commercial jars are not strong enough to be safely used for repeated home canning. Mason jars—which screw shut with a threaded neck—are the most common choice.

Is it okay to reuse the lids?

After a lid has been pried off a jar once, a perfect fit can no longer be guaranteed. The jars themselves can be used many times, as long as the sealing rims are perfectly smooth and there are no scratches or cracks. Yes, this book is about saving money on home canning, but the metal lid is one area where you don't want to cut corners. Invest in new lids every time you home can.

What is botulism?

Botulism is a serious, often fatal form of food poisoning. The poison is produced by *Clostridium botulinum*, a bacterium that is found everywhere—in soil, on raw fruits and vegetables, and on meat and fish. Over the years, a number of people have died from botulism as a direct result of improper home canning. It is not something to take lightly.

What causes botulism?

Botulism spores are resistant to heat—even from boiling water—and thrive in a moist, oxygen-free environment. They are most commonly found in low-acid foods like vegetables and meat. They can only be killed at temperatures over 240 degrees. Water boils at a much lower temperature, and you will need to pressure can these low-acid foods in order for them to be safe. As botulism spores reproduce, they generate one of the most extraordinarily powerful poisons on earth: one teaspoon worth of the spore is sufficient to kill 100,000 people. Improper home canning creates the perfect environment in which to grow the botulism toxin. Because food contaminated by botulism may very well look and smell normal, there

is often no warning. That is why home canning must be done properly with extreme care—any shortcuts you take could be deadly. Now do you understand why canning safety is important?

What should you do if the home-canned food doesn't look right?

Never eat, or even taste, any home-canned food that appears to be spoiled (gray or moldy), foams, or develops a bad smell during cooking. Stay away if the container has a bulging lid or is leeching or you are not sure whether the food was properly canned.

How do I dispose of the product in question?

1. Place any questionable containers and food in a waterproof container and throw it in the garbage.

2. Do not feed the questionable food to your pets or any other animals.

3. After throwing it away, wash your hands well with warm, soapy water. Also, wash any utensils or surfaces the food or container may have touched.

What is basic sanitation and the importance of cleanliness?

The big safety factor to keep in mind is cleanliness. All work surfaces should be kept clean during all stages of the canning process. The food being preserved must itself be rinsed clean. It is particularly important to sterilize the jars and seals before use. Basic sanitation is the single most important factor in safety for home canning. Don't skimp on this step.

How do I sterilize jars?

Completely submerse canning jars in boiling water for 10 minutes. If you live at higher elevations (over 1,000 feet), allow one minute more of boiling for each extra 1,000 feet of elevation. To sterilize tops (seals with rubber gaskets), simmer them for five minutes. It is important not to boil the lids or the rubber will become too soft and may start to come off the metal.

Any questions?

Home canning is perfectly safe . . . but it needs to be done correctly. I recommend that you read up on home canning before you try it. Good books are available on the subject (like the one you're holding now). If you have an older pressure canner and cannot find the instructions, contact the manufacturer to ask for a copy.

Can home-canned food spoil?

I get asked this question often. "Can my home-canned food spoil?" I've been to many canning seminars. At one such seminar, a keynote speaker (who was a seasoned home canner) started telling everyone in the audience that she had home-canned food in her pantry that was over ten years old and they were still eating it. She said, "I haven't killed anyone yet." I wanted to throw a book at her. Despite her intention of trying to tell people that home canning was safe, she was actually leading them down a very dangerous and potentially lethal path. Home-canned food can spoil. Anyone who says differently doesn't have a real vested interest in your family's health. Saving money is one thing, but endangering yourself is another. Throwing away food because you're not sure of its safety may cost you a little money, but it could save a life! Educate yourself. You'll be so glad you did.

Here is a list of common causes for spoil-factors in home-canned food products—and solutions that will fix the problems:

Poor quality fresh food or food that is unwashed, unpeeled, or untrimmed

Many microorganisms grow on vegetable skins, and improper removal of this part of the plant can cause problems. This results in a high microbial load. That is bad because it may need a longer processing time to kill all the evil little micro-dudes in there.

Fix it: Prepare food properly according to the recipe directions. I know it takes time, but it is worth the effort. Use only the freshest, most beautiful produce and the best quality you can find. The best price on these items will always be found when they are in season. Trim. Peel.

Food packed too tightly

This mistake is very common with first-time home canning. I made this mistake once myself. I thought it would be a good idea to cram the jar as full as possible with peaches. There was very little room for the syrup. After processing, the jar sealed fine, but a week or two later, the peaches were discolored and the jar was oozing. Learn from my mistake. Don't overpack your jars. Your effort to put a lot of food in the jar can insulate the food in the center of the jar from getting hot enough for complete sterilization.

Fix it: Pack food loosely. Prepare according to the USDA Guidelines (½-inch slices, halves, and so on), and then use the recommended time, pressure, and temperature.

Jars sat too long before processing

If processing is not started right after the jars are filled and their lids are placed on them, microorganisms may grow to very high levels before processing. This happens a lot if you are canning a large amount of food at one time.

Fix it: Fill jars as quickly as possible and use sterile equipment. Process in a timely manner. Take the time to do it right. This means you may have to invest in a second or even third canner or borrow one from a friend. This will speed up the process and you won't be left with jars that sat long enough to start making a lot of bacteria.

Didn't heat process long enough

This can happen if there is a power failure or pressure fluctuation or by not starting your timer at the correct moment. You also may be using an inaccurate heat-processing recommendation time.

Fix it: Check to be sure you're using up-to-date processing times. Things may be different than they were several years ago when your grandmother was canning. Watch closely to be sure processing isn't interrupted. Always start your timer when water comes to a full rolling boil for water-bath canning. Start your timer for pressure canning only after the canner has come to full pressure.

Old-school canning methods or canning fads that are NOT safe were used

Open-kettle jam-canning recipes in older cookbooks will tell you that it is okay to boil your jam, ladle it into hot jars, and then seal it tight without water-bath processing. This method is not considered safe because bacteria can grow on the lids. Think about it. If you touch the lid after touching something with germs and then put that on your jar, you've just exposed the jar to problems. I also have a few friends who were taught that open-kettle canning was okay if they turned the jars upside down after sealing them. I have no idea why that would make it better for safety. It might make the jam dizzy, but it certainly won't make it safe.

Fix it: Heat-process your jars, darlings!

Microwave canning or oven canning methods were used.

Again, these fad methods do not get the canned food hot enough long enough to kill microorganisms. I've seen many posts on the internet about "home canning butter" where the butter is melted in jars in the oven and then topped with a lid. Some are doing the same with cheese. This is incredibly unsafe! There is not a proven safe method for home canning butter or fresh cheese. If world-renowned university food science departments can't give you a proper processing time that is proven to be safe, what makes you think that someone on the internet without a lab to test the safety is right? Do not be fooled.

Fix it: Use recommended canning methods. Use a pressure canner for low-acid foods and a boiling water-bath canner for high-acid foods.

Improperly cooled jars

Jars left in the canner at the end of processing time or when the gauge reads "0" can be a problem. As jars cool, they can suck water (containing microbes or spores) back into the jar with the food. Very slow and very rapid cooling can interfere with seal formation.

Fix it: Remove jars from the canner after processing to cool and protect from extreme temperatures.

Use of paraffin to seal jelly jars

My grandma used to melt wax and put it on top of her hot jelly and jams. Don't be offended when I say this: Sorry, Grandma. Paraffin is no longer recommended for sealing jams, jellies, or preserves. Mold, which is the most common spoiler of sweet spreads, can send "roots" down along the edge of the paraffin and produce toxic substances and junk in the spread. Mmm. Germ jam.

Fix it: Can and process your jams, jellies, and preserves as you would other foods.

food-borne illness and home canning

Once you know what is safe, you are on your way!

Don't join the FBI—it could kill you. I don't mean the Feds. I am talking about food-borne illness. Here are a few things you need to know about the most common culprits in home-canning disasters. If it is predictable, it is totally preventable. In this case, there are some things you should know. Be alert and aware. Don't panic. Just know the facts.

Intoxication: Food can contain toxins produced during a pathogen's life. Once in the body, these toxins act as poison (see staphylococcus and botulism).

Infection: Food can also contain a large number of living pathogens. These multiply in the body and usually attack the gastrointestinal lining (salmonellosis).

Chemical poisoning: In home canning, chemical poisoning can be caused by improper washing of fruits and vegetables if you buy commercially or raise your own. Use food-grade or organic vegetables and fruits and wash them! Dish soap is usually enough. You can't cook off a chemical poison, so even the proper heating and canning process won't get rid of this kind of FBI!

my biggest concerns in home canning

Botulism

12 to 36-hour incubation period.

Symptoms: Sore throat, vomiting, blurred vision, cramps, difficulty breathing, central nervous system damage, and possible paralysis. The fatality rate is 70 percent! Spores are hard to detect because they have no smell or flavor. The spores also have a high resistance to heat and need to be boiled 20–25 minutes to die. They can be found in soil.

Prevention: Wash your fruits and vegetables! Peel potatoes. Pressure can low-acid foods (meats, vegetables). Always use approved recipes for water-bath canning.

Staphylococcus

2 to 4-hour incubation period

Symptoms: Vomiting, cramps, diarrhea, and nausea. This is a facultative bacteria found in the nose, throat, and skin of infected humans. The toxins cannot be destroyed by heat!

Preventions: People with infected cuts or burns or with respiratory illness should not handle food. Wear gloves, and don't home can when you feel sick. You may not know you have a staph infection! This is also a good way to get out of helping Granny snap beans to put in canning jars.

Plant and animal poison

Alkaloids and organic acids are a big concern. The most common in home canning are rhubarb leaves.

Symptoms: Nausea, vomiting, and diarrhea.

Prevention: Remove rhubarb leaves well and wash all surfaces.

Salmonellosis

6 to 48-hour incubation period

Symptoms: Headache, diarrhea, cramps, and fever. It can be fatal or lead to arthritis, meningitis, and typhoid. This illness grows in the intestines of humans and can be killed at temperatures over 165 degrees. Boiling is 212 degrees!

Prevention: Eliminate all flies in your home before canning. Send the kids running around with a fly-swatter. Wash hands and sanitize . . . even under fingernails! This especially applies after using the bathroom or changing the baby. Be sure when canning to not use utensils that have come in contact with meat (unless pressure canning).

my biggest sanitation tips

» Use of a sanitation solution or a food-grade kitchen sanitizer for all cutting surfaces is highly acceptable.

» It is extremely important to have strict personal sanitation during canning sessions!

» Keep jars and lids hot and sterile.

» Keep your hair tied back. It makes you look sassy, and it keeps hair out of your food.

» Wear gloves and an apron that you don't take in the bathroom! Do I even have to tell you that?

» Cook only in boiling water (not just baby bubbles) the full amount of time.

» If you pressure can, follow the rules given by the manufacturer of your canner.

» If your spouse or children help you with the canning, make sure they obey the sanitation rules.

classifications of foods & processing methods

The acidity of food
For home canning, foods are divided into two classifications: acid foods and low-acid foods. The acidity of food (pH level) will ultimately determine which method of safe processing you use for the products.

High-acid foods (and acid-added foods)
High-acid foods are foods naturally high in acid or that have had acid added to increase the pH level. Lemon juice, citric acid, and vinegar labeled 5% acidity are added to recipes to increase acidity. The boiling water method is used for these foods and can be used as long as they have a pH level of 4.6 or less. Most fruits and sweet spreads are classified high acid. Tomatoes and figs require additional acid so they may be canned using a water-bath canner. Some low-acid foods, like cucumbers and cabbage, are treated with acid to make pickles and sauerkraut and can still be classified as high-acid products. Again, the pH level must be 4.6 or less for this to be true. High-acid foods need to have heat processing in order to kill natural enzymes and any yeast or molds. This will happen in temperatures over 140 degrees and in the boiling water-bath process.

What is the "boiling water-bath" processing method?
The "boiling water-bath" is probably what you saw your mother or grandmother doing. It involves dropping a basket of sealed jars into a large pot of rapidly boiling water.

Things to know about water-bath canning
» Remove excess air in the jars using a canning tool so that the expansion of air in the jar during the processing will not cause the jar to burst.

» Keep jars on a rack so water can circulate around them.

» Never place jars directly on the bottom of the pot. The heat will make them crack.

» Bring water to a full rolling boil, at least an inch over the lids of the jars.

» Start counting your "processing time" only after the water in the canner comes to a full rolling boil. The temperature at which water boils at sea level is 212 degrees. This temperature must be maintained for the full processing time in order to destroy yeast, molds, and bacteria.

Low-acid foods
There are foods that are low in acid naturally. Meats, most vegetables, and seafood are in this group. Most soups, hearty stews, and meat sauces are also classified as a low-acid food because they have a combination of ingredients. Some salsas, if the onion content is too high, can be considered low-acid foods. Any foods with a pH level higher than 4.6 are called low-acid foods and must be heated to a high enough temperature to kill botulism spores as well as all the toxins they produce. Pressure canning allows the temperature in the jars to exceed what could happen in boiling water. Remember, botulism spores die at 240 degrees and water boils at 212 degrees at sea level. You cannot boil them longer to replace the

pressure-canning method. Ever. Investing in a pressure canner was one of the best things I ever did for saving money and home canning, but it does require a little more time and patience than water-bath canning.

What is pressure canning?

A pressure canner is a large cast-aluminum pot with a locking lid and a pressure gauge. By cooking under pressure, you can bring the temperature of jars up to 240 degrees F (116 degrees C). This is the minimum temperature necessary to destroy botulism spores and the only way to guarantee safe canning for food items such as vegetables, meats, and seafood. Your pressure canner should come with complete instructions. Always follow them carefully.

For years I was afraid to use a pressure cooker or canner. I somehow imagined that one day my pressure cooker would explode and I'd die in a vicious vortex of stew-meat with hot beans lodged in my eyes. Repeat after me: "When operated correctly, they are perfectly safe." I chant that phrase every day, whenever the thought of exploding canners enters my mind. They really are safe. As a random side note, I also chant "They are perfectly safe" when I go on an escalator as well. Baby steps, darlings. Baby steps.

Keep these pointers in mind

» Ten pounds is the minimum safe pressure.

» Processing time will vary depending on the type of food being preserved and the size of the jar. Never shorten the cooking time that is recommended in the instructions.

» If you live more than 1,000 feet above sea level, then both the pressure and cooking time will have to be adjusted (consult the chart on the following page).

» Once the right pressure is reached during cooking, it must be kept constant throughout the cooking step.

» Both weighted gauges and dial gauges should be checked for accuracy.

» Read the manufacturer's directions carefully for recommended testing/frequency procedures to make sure your canner is being operated safely and correctly.

altitude

Barometric pressure is a big deal in the world of food canning. Pressure is reduced at higher altitudes, and this will affect the temperature at which water boils. After all that we have discussed about getting the temperature hot enough to kill bacteria, it just stands to reason that you need to adjust the processing time at a higher altitude in order to make sure all those bad boys are killed off. This applies for both water-bath canning and pressure canning. There are adjustments if you live up in the mountains. Not sure? Check with your local university extension office. They can tell you how high you are—in altitude, not in the drug world. I have no idea how high you are right now. I don't want to know.

boiling water canner altitude adjustments[1]

Altitude in Feet	Increase Processing Time
1,001–3,000	5 minutes
3,001–6,000	10 minutes
6,001–8,000	15 minutes
8,001–10,000	20 minutes

pressure canner altitude adjustments[1]

Altitude in Feet	Weighted Gauge	Dial Gauge
0–1000	10	11
1,001–2,000	15	11
2,001–4,000	15	12
4,001–6,000	15	13
6,001–8,000	15	14
8,001–10,000	15	15

[1]Ball Blue Book guide to preserving, p. 5.

equipment

Food preservation equipment has come a long way since my grandmother was canning foods. In my dramatic mind, I sometimes picture her in her little kitchen as I bring in boxes of the best new modern tools. She was a very simple and modest woman, but I think she'd be as thrilled as I have been to see the changes for the better that have happened in home canning. She'd also ask me why I still insist on not keeping my bedroom tidy. That, of course, has nothing to do with home canning. If you find yourself in this situation, employ a diversionary tactic at this point and show Granny something new and shiny for her canning shenanigans. "Canning Shenanigans" is also going to be the name of my euro-retro-folk-country band. That, of course, also has nothing to do with home canning.

There are a lot of simple new gadgets to ease you into this new way of life, and some of them are very budget-friendly. Some are not inexpensive, but they are an investment if you plan on home canning for a very long portion of your life. One of my favorite companies for this has long been Ball®. They recently have come out with some outstanding home conversion packs that will turn almost any heavy pot into a home water-bath canner and also some fully automated pressure canning systems for smaller batches. I personally use the All American® pressure canner and the Presto® pressure canner for my low-acid processing. I'm still waiting for the handy tool that will help me keep my bedroom tidy and double as a banjo for the band.

On canning days, I keep on hand . . .

Canning funnels. They come in all kinds of colors and styles. I prefer red ones. That is the true and righteous color for all kitchen equipment. I'm kidding. The color of the funnel doesn't matter. It is what goes through the funnel that counts.

Mason jars. These are the commercially made jars designed to withstand the pressure and heat of home canning methods. They come in a great variety of sizes and shapes. Each recipe is very specific on the processing times for each jar size. Please do not alter the processing times.

New metal lids and clean rings. These metal lids are part of the two pieces of the canning lid. They have a rubber seal that is heated and forms itself to the ring of the jar. They are designed to be used only once and cannot be reused. Once a jar is opened, plan on throwing that part away instead of using it for future canning projects, or find a fun way to recycle them in art projects. I use them for dangly retro earrings. Okay, I don't actually do that. The metal rings that are used to keep the lid tight to the jar can be reused, as long as they are free from rust or corrosion. Once they get rusty, they're great for disco-night bracelets, but not for canning.

Magnetic stick/lid-wand. This is a plastic stick with a magnet lodged in its end that is valuable in taking the lids out of simmering water without touching the lid with your fingers. This is a fantastic tool for keeping the lid from being damaged, which sometimes happens when using a fork or sharp object. It is also a handy tool for retrieving hot-wheels from under the refrigerator. I've done that.

Jar clamps/jar lifters. I sometimes joke that these are clamps that could be used to deliver a baby. I'd never really use them for that purpose . . . unless I had nothing better to use. They are rubber-coated metal clamps that are rounded on the clamp end to be able to hold the rims of jars and lower jars into boiling water. Only once did I try to remove jars from boiling water without a jar clamp/lifter, and it was the most frustration I've ever had in the kitchen. I'd pay for the video of that experience. I'd make a million bucks on YouTube. Invest in a set. You'll be glad you did so.

Wire racks. I cool my jars on wire bakery racks. You can also use clean towels. I just prefer having the racks because of the even airflow around the jars. There are round wire racks that can be used to convert larger pots to water-bath canners as well.

Plastic knives. In canning, the removal of excess air trapped in pockets inside the jar is pivotal in keeping the jars from rupturing during the processing step. In order to do this, a plastic nonreactive tool (like a plastic knife) is used to slide between the jar and the product packed inside the jar. This displacement of air bubbles is necessary. Plastic won't react to acid as a metal knife might. This will keep your flavors true and keep metal from leaching into your food. They are also a great tool to take on a picnic, but not a great tool to replace a Popsicle stick in your homemade pudding pops. That of course has nothing to do with home canning and everything to do with not being an idiot.

Headspace measuring tool. It will be important how much room is in the headspace of your jar. This airspace will be specific with each recipe. Keep the proper space for heat expansion. This will keep jars from bursting during the heating process. It will also help measure gnome mohawks to be sure they are at wrestling regulation length. Seriously, if you are seeing little gnomes in spandex wrestle, there will not be any home canning for you today. They will be checking your personal headspace for other, more serious issues.

Surface sanitizer. I am a nerd about this stuff, but if I'm working with meat or higher protein foods, I'm obsessive about making sure I sanitize my work surfaces. It is better to be over cautious than relaxed when it comes to surface sanitizing. Make sure you use food-grade sanitizer or a low amount of bleach in water (about 1 tablespoon to every 5 gallons). Don't go all "OCD-crazy" and use an electric toothbrush to sanitize your counters, just make sure things are clean.

Hand sanitizer/rubber gloves. Use these when working with foods to keep them sanitary. If you have any cuts on your fingers or hands, always use rubber gloves. Unless, of course, you just cut your finger completely off and need to go to the hospital. A rubber glove won't help at that point. Just run away screaming and get that digit reattached.

Clean towels and dishcloths. These are essential for keeping germs from spreading. Once a towel has been used to wipe a surface with meat or poultry, do not use it to clean a surface where you plan on chopping vegetables or fruit. Yikes. Chicken guts and junk. This is called "cross-contamination" and it is just evil. There. I said it. Evil.

Hot pads/gloves. These are necessary when handling hot jars. I prefer pads and gloves made from silicon because they can be easily sanitized between uses. They also double well as Halloween alien-invasion costume props.

Labels/permanent markers. You need to properly ensure you're keeping things used and rotated within the recommended one year after processing. Date items clearly. You can get as "Martha Stewart" as you want on labels, but mine are usually pretty short and sweet and written on the lid of the jar after it cools.

Measuring cups and spoons. For proper pH in your jars, follow the recipes precisely. Don't estimate, especially when it comes to the proportions of additional acid used in your recipes. My husband used to tell me that there was a measuring cup in every new laundry soap box. I know there are indeed measuring cups in every new laundry soap box. Just don't use it for measuring sugar . . . unless you want lemony-fresh jam.

A kitchen scale. Use a scale to weigh fruit and other ingredients whenever possible. Again, this will ensure there is the proper pH in your recipe. As a random side note, kitchen scales are too small to weigh yourself after eating too many chocolate-covered cinnamon bears. I will not ever make that mistake again.

pH strips. These are available at many restaurant supply stores and in canning departments at some specialty stores. These are optional if you follow the recipes precisely. When in doubt, use a pH strip.

An accurate kitchen timer. Use a timer for every single processing time. Get one that works for you. This will also be a good tool when Mom needs a "time out."

Food processors, pitting tools, slicers, juice extractors, and more. All of these can be used to make your work go faster when processing a lot of produce. Some are worth the investment if you plan on doing a lot of canning. Some are not. Use your own judgment. I bought a cherry pitter because I was doing bushels and bushels of cherries every season. If I had only 5 or 6 jars to do, I would have just used a smaller, less expensive, hand-sized pitter. The same can be said of apple slicer machines and so forth. Make this work for your budget, not against it. All of these tools are also very fun to use on play-dough day. Just be sure to get the green dough out of the juice extractor before making grape juice. That would be horrible.

Broadway showtunes and chocolate-covered cinnamon bears . . . Oh wait. Those are from my personal list of things to always have in the kitchen on canning day. The music keeps me dancing like Ginger Rogers and the cinnamon bears make me fabu-beautiful. Don't judge me.

it is a total process

Heat processing is 100% necessary, and in this book the times and processes are not interchangeable. If I specify water-bath time, it cannot be switched to pressure canning time (and vice versa). These processing times are also based on the sizes of the jars, pH levels of the food, and how the food is packed in the jars. The procedures, when followed correctly, will get the jar contents hot enough to kill enzyme activity and destroy microorganisms.

Boiling water processing procedure

1. Half-fill the water canner and bring to a simmer (180 degrees). Put canning rack over the water.

2. Follow recipe preparation and fill jars as directed. Tighten lids (hand-tight).

3. Immediately after jars are filled, place them in the canning rack and carefully lower the canning rack into the water. Make sure the water level is 1–2 inches above the jars by adding boiling water if needed.

4. Put lid on the canner. Increase heat and bring to a rolling boil. Once water is boiling, set timer and retain rolling boil for the full processing time.

5. When processing is complete, remove from heat and take off the lid of the canner. Cool the canner 5 minutes prior to removing jars from the water.

6. Take the jars from the canner and place upright on a dry towel, cooling rack, or cutting board, allowing 1–2 inches of wiggle-space between each jar (for air circulation). DON'T tighten the bands when they are still warm! Jars may burst if you do so! Allow your jars to cool 12–24 hours before messing around with them. This gives the seals time to set. When they have cooled, check the rings and retighten if needed.

Pressure processing procedure

1. Carefully place canning rack in the bottom of the pressure canner and fill water level to 2 inches (or whatever your model of canner specifies). Heat to a simmering 180 degrees and hold the temperature and water level.

2. Follow recipe preparations and fill jars as directed, carefully measuring headspace and using the air-removing tool to release any air inside the jar. Top with sterilized jar lids and rings. Tighten the rings.

3. Place jars on rack inside of the pressure canner. Lock lid in place according to your specific canner's specifications. Leave the weight off the top vent or open the petcock. At this point, set your stove to medium-high heat until the steam just flows in an even stream from the vent pipe or petcock. Exhaust the steam from the canner for 10 solid minutes.

4. Place the weight on the vent or close the pet-cock. If you've done it correctly, the canner should reach pressure in 5 minutes or less. When the gauge reaches the pressure you need, start your timer and adjust the heat on your stove to medium-high or whatever temperature is necessary to maintain the pressure for the whole processing time.

5. When the time is up, turn off your heat and remove the canner from the heat. Allow it to cool naturally (that means don't remove the weight or do anything), just let it sit there until the pressure is at zero. Let it cool an additional 10 minutes and then remove the lid to let the steam escape. Wait another 10 minutes and then remove the jars.

6. Take the jars from the canner and place upright on a dry towel, cooling rack, or cutting board, allowing 1–2 inches of wiggle-space between each jar (for air circulation). DON'T tighten the bands when they are still warm! Jars may burst if you do so! Cool in an area free from any draft for 12–24 hours. Jars will make a "ping" sound as the lids are sealing. You'll start to look for that sound as music to your ears.

cooling and testing

When all the processing is complete and the jars have set for 12–24 hours, check them out for proper sealing.

Check the rings. Are the rings in need of tightening? I take the rings off, clean the rings and rims of the jar with a warm moist towel, allow them to dry, and then retighten the rings on my jars. This ensures there isn't any product that leaked out of the jar during processing to fester between the lid and ring. This is not a necessary step, and rings don't need to be put back on the jars at all. I just like having them on my jars.

Tap the lids to be sure they sealed correctly. They should not make a popping sound when pressure is applied to the top of the jar.

Reprocess if necessary. Sometimes a few jars will not seal correctly. It is very important that those jars be either reprocessed by removing the lids, reheating the product and reprocessing with a new lid according to the recipe directions, OR placed in the fridge to be used in a few days.

If the jar didn't seal because the jar was damaged, don't eat it. Dispose of it properly.

storage and use of home-canned goods

Improper storage

Heat: Arizona in the summer is the perfect example of the most evil place to store jars. I love my desert home, but it is hard in the summer to find a cool place to store all my treasures. Home-canned foods that are exposed to temperatures over 95 degrees F may spoil. It is the perfect breeding temperature for junk. Storing home-canned food products in the garage isn't a good idea, especially in warm climates. Microorganisms tolerate and will grow at high temperatures. So, if they are still present, they may grow and spoil the food, or alter the food so that other microorganisms can grow.

Sunlight: You want to show off your homemaking skills, so you line the jars up in your kitchen window. Great. You'll look good for a while. Home-canned foods stored in the sunlight may get very hot inside, which allows the air in the headspace to expand, breaking open the seal and allowing microorganisms and recontamination the food. What will the neighbors say about those moldy jars then?

Acid leaks: I've seen this one a lot with pickles and very acidic foods (pickled or fermented products and some juices). If these were kept for a long time, the acid may have eaten away at the lid, resulting in pinholes that allowed microorganisms to get into the jar. Discard any home-canned food with damaged or flaking metal on the lid.

Rustic isn't a good thing. I love the rustic look, but lids on home-canned foods stored in a damp place may also rust through, allowing microbes to get into the food. Yikes. Save the rustic look for the family cabin.

Solution: Store home-canned foods in a cool, dry place. Date all home-canned goods and use within a year. Use old rusty canning rings for jingle-jangle girlie bracelets. All the cool girls are wearing them.

Use it or lose it: When you've used proper canning procedures and modern methods, there isn't any question as to your canned food being safe. This being said, it is always a good idea to visually inspect each jar before you use them. Make sure there isn't any visible sign of fermentation or mold.

The USDA recommends boiling home-canned foods for 10 minutes before serving them. Baking things in a pie counts.

Use good judgment: If it looks or smells spoiled, don't eat it. Don't feed it to your pets.

Rotate and use home-canned products within a year of home canning.

Once opened, store in the fridge, as you would any commercially canned foods.

references

Due to the nature and safety of home canning, I have used only canning processing times and methods that have been approved by the USDA for safe home canning. The processing times and general guidelines are found in many locations, but I used the sources to the right as my primary references.

» *Complete Guide to Home Canning*, Agriculture Information Bulletin No. 539, USDA (revised 2009).

» The USDA home canning website: http://nchfp.uga.edu/index.html.

» *Ball® Blue Book Guide to Preserving*, Hearthmark, LLC dba Jarden Home Brands (2011).

» FreshPreserving.com, by Ball® Corporation.

where to find specialty canning products

FreshPreserving.com

This website had many reference locations, as well as a comprehensive online store for purchase of their specialty products.

Specialty canning jars

JarStore.com

FillMoreContainer.com

Pressure canners

AllAmericanCanner.com

Presto.com

chapter two

high-acid foods

These apples, simmered slowly in a spicy cinnamon syrup, are unlike any other. They are excellent over pancakes or waffles. Use them in apple crisps or cobblers. They are perfect for a spicy tart or pie.

apples in cinnamon syrup

Yields about 6 pints

9–10 lbs. tart apples, peeled, sliced into eighths

½ cup lemon juice

1½ cups sugar

1 cup apple cider vinegar (5% acidity)

½ tsp. natural hot cinnamon oil (for candy making)

1½ tsp. ground clove

1 Tbsp. minced candied ginger

2 cups water

⅔ cup non-GMO corn syrup

1. Place peeled, sliced apples in a large bowl and toss with lemon juice to prevent browning. Combine remaining ingredients in a large pot and bring to a slow simmer. Add apples and simmer for five minutes.

2. Pack into hot sterile jars with a ½-inch headspace and fill with hot syrup over the apples. Again, be sure to leave a ½-inch headspace. Slide non-metallic knife down sides of jar to remove air. Top with two-piece lid and seal tightly. Process for 15 minutes in a boiling water canner. Transfer to a clean dry cloth or cooling rack out of the way of any draft. Allow to cool 12 hours before moving jars.

Money-saving tip: Buy apples that are in season, tart, and firm. It should cost around $2.50 for the apples at the right time of year. Use bottled lemon juice to ensure proper acidity. If I already have the jars and basic ingredients like sugar and vinegar on hand, these apples cost about 75 cents a jar to produce.

No combination could be better than warm vanilla and nutmeg mingled with tart apples. These baking apples are sure to invoke all the feelings of homespun goodness. Use them in any recipe that you'd use apples in. Our family favorite is using them in apple fritters or folded into homemade frozen yogurt.

baking apples with vanilla bean and nutmeg

Yields 4 quarts or 8 pints

11–12 lbs. tart Granny Smith apples, cored, peeled, and cut into ¾-inch slices

½ cup lemon juice

1 cup sugar

2 cups water

1 Tbsp. vanilla bean paste (specialty food stores) or double-strength vanilla

1 tsp. fresh ground nutmeg

1. Place peeled and sliced apples in a large bowl and toss with lemon juice to prevent browning. Combine remaining ingredients in a large pot and bring to a slow simmer. Add apples and simmer for 5 minutes.

2. Pack into hot sterile jars with a ½-inch headspace. Fill with hot syrup over the apples. Again, be sure to leave a ½-inch headspace. Slide non-metallic knife down sides of jar to remove air. Top with two-piece lid and seal tightly. Process 20 minutes in a boiling water canner. Transfer to a clean dry cloth or cooling rack out of the way of any draft. Allow to cool 12 hours before moving jars.

Money-saving tip: Buy apples that are in season, tart, and firm. It should cost around $5 for the apples at the right time of year. Use bottled lemon juice to ensure proper acidity. If I already have the jars and basic ingredients like sugar and lemon juice on hand, these apples cost about $1.25 a jar to produce.

Anyone who knows me knows that my favorite berry is a luscious, ripe blackberry. I could eat them all day until I was found in a pool of berry juice with streaks of purple on my cheeks. Needless to say, this berry is awesome for home canning, and when coupled with a hint of spice and brandy (or brandy flavor), it is the most delicate and delightful combination ever. I serve them over vanilla ice cream or pound cake or both. When canning berries, you'll need to get them as ripe and fresh as possible.

blackberries and brandy

Yields 2 quarts or 4 pints

4 lbs. blackberries, washed

2 cups sugar

2 cups water

2 tsp. brandy flavor extract (or ¼ cup brandy)

① Wash your berries, drain well, and pack into jars loosely. In a separate medium pot, combine the sugar, water, and brandy or brandy flavor. Simmer the sugar mixture until the crystals of sugar are dissolved into the water. Pour the hot syrup over the berries to cover them; leave ½-inch headspace. Remove any air bubbles.

② Adjust two-piece cap and process in a boiling water-bath canner for 20 minutes for quart jars and 15 minutes for pint jars. Transfer to a clean dry cloth or cooling rack out of the way of any draft. Allow to cool 12 hours before moving jars.

Money-saving tip: Purchase berries in season and look for specials at the farmer's market. This will cut costs dramatically. Previously frozen blackberries can be used to cut costs, but they must be defrosted first and will lose their shape dramatically.

When my babies were small, I didn't go a single day without opening a jar of applesauce. Making our own not only saved money, it ensured my kids got the very best! The addition of ginger adds a remarkable flavor and aids in digestion.

gingered caramel applesauce

Yields 3 quarts or 6 pints

9 lbs. apples (about 3 lbs. apples per quart jar)

water

1 Tbsp. ground ginger

1 Tbsp. vanilla

2 cups brown sugar (optional)

1. Peel, core, and cut apples. Simmer in large pot with ginger and just enough water to keep the apples and ginger from sticking to the pan. Purée cooked apples in a food processor or strong blender. Add brown sugar if desired.

2. Return to pot and keep at boiling temperature when filling jars. Leave ½-inch headspace. Tighten two-piece lids on jars. Process 20 minutes for pints and quarts in boiling water canner. Transfer to a clean, dry cloth or cooling rack out of the way of any draft. Allow to cool 12 hours before moving jars.

Money-saving tip: Buy apples that are in season, tart, and firm. It should cost around $2.50 for the apples at the right time of year. Cost per pint: about 50 cents.

Using maple syrup as the liquid for canning apricots has been a family tradition for many years at my home. When these apricots are draped over warm, fluffy waffles or spiced pancakes, the flavor is out of this world! They are excellent for apricot cobblers and anywhere you wish to have a delicious breakfast addition.

maple apricots

Yields 4 quarts or 8 pints

8–10 lbs. fresh apricots, seeded and cut in half

1 cup maple syrup

2 cups sugar

3 cups water

½ tsp. fresh ground nutmeg

1. Pack apricots, cavity side down, into canning jars. In a large pot combine the syrup, sugar, water, and nutmeg. Simmer until the sugar is dissolved. Ladle the hot syrup over the apricots. Remove air bubbles. Leave ½-inch headspace.

2. Top with two-piece canning lids and seal tightly. Process pints 25 minutes and quarts 30 minutes in a boiling water-bath canner. Transfer to a clean, dry cloth or cooling rack out of the way of any draft. Allow to cool 12 hours before moving jars.

Money-saving tip: Apricots are very seasonal. Watch the cost carefully or find a friend with an overabundant crop on their apricot tree. It should cost around $8.00 for the apricots at the right time of year. Real maple syrup is going to cost a bit more than the fake table syrup. Total cost: about $12.00 to produce. If I already have the lids and canning jars, the cost per pint is about $1.50 or $3.00 a quart. If money is tight and you don't mind using pancake syrup instead of real maple syrup, the cost will go down quite a bit per jar.

I've used these home-canned blueberries for the most remarkable blueberry muffins on earth! The flavor of the berries is bursting with a nuance of the amaretto that cannot be beat! Try these berries folded into your favorite yogurt or cascaded in bubbles of blue over your most beautiful cheesecakes. You'll love it!

blueberries amaretto

Yields 2 quarts or 4 pints

4 lbs. blueberries, washed

2 cups sugar

2 cups water

2 tsp. almond flavor extract (or ¼-cup amaretto liqueur)

1. Wash your berries and pack into jars loosely. In a separate medium pot, combine the sugar, water, and almond flavor or amaretto. Simmer the sugar mixture until the crystals of sugar are dissolved into the water.

2. Pour the hot syrup over the berries to cover them, leaving a ½-inch headspace. Remove any air bubbles. Adjust two-piece cap and process in a boiling water-bath canner for 20 minutes on quart jars and 15 minutes for pint jars. Transfer to a clean, dry cloth or cooling rack out of the way of any draft. Allow to cool 12 hours before moving jars.

Money-saving tip: Purchase berries in season and look for specials at the farmer's market. This will cut costs dramatically. Previously frozen blueberries can be used to cut costs, but they must be defrosted first and will lose their shape dramatically.

Once you make your own cranberry sauce, you'll never want to have that other jelly stuff again. The cranberries are whole and juicy and perfectly tart-sweet with just the right subtle nuance of spice. We stock up on the bags of fresh berries when they are in season, as the price goes down dramatically. The sauce is a thoughtful gift for the holiday season and the perfect flavor to complement any turkey or roasted meat.

spiced whole cranberries in sauce

Yields about 12 pints

16 cups cranberries

8 cups sugar

8 cups water

1 Tbsp. ground ginger

1 Tbsp. ground cinnamon

1 Tbsp. orange oil*

1. Wash and drain the cranberries. Combine the sugar, water, and spices in a large pot and simmer until sugar is dissolved. Add the clean cranberries to the sugar mixture and simmer without stirring until skins pop and burst, about 15 minutes.

2. Spoon the hot cranberries into sterilized jars, allowing ½-inch headspace in the jars. Top each jar with warmed canning lids and tighten. Place jars in a boiling water-bath. Process 15 minutes.

Money-saving tip: If you already have the canning jars, these are less than a dollar to make per jar if cranberries are purchased during their season. If you purchase frozen berries, defrost before turning them into this cranberry sauce.

*Orange oil is the concentrated essential oil extracted from the orange zest and is available in health food stores.

During the holidays, there is nothing more comforting than a mixed berry cobbler baked using these remarkable mulled mixed berries. Save a few jars for giving to your best friends, or better yet, serve them to your family!

mulled mixed berries

Yields 2 quarts or 4 pints

1 lb. blackberries, washed

1 lb. blueberries, washed

2 lbs. raspberries, washed

2 cups sugar

2 cups water

2 tsp. rum flavor extract (or ¼ cup rum)

1 tsp. ground cinnamon

½ tsp. ground cardamom

½ tsp. ground allspice

¼ tsp. anise seed

1. Wash your berries, mix together, and pack into jars loosely. In a separate medium pot, combine the sugar, water, and remaining ingredients. Simmer the sugar mixture until the crystals of sugar are dissolved into the water. Pour the hot syrup over the berries to cover them, leaving a ½-inch headspace. Remove any air bubbles.

2. Adjust two-piece cap and process in a boiling water-bath canner for 20 minutes for quart jars and 15 minutes for pint jars. Transfer to a clean, dry cloth or cooling rack out of the way of any draft. Allow to cool 12 hours before moving jars.

Money-saving tip: Purchase berries in season and look for specials at the farmer's market. This will cut costs dramatically. Previously frozen berries can be used to cut costs, but they must be defrosted first and will lose their shape dramatically.

When you home can cherries, adding a sugar syrup will make them perfect for pies and pastries and anywhere you want some cherry notes. These vanilla cherries are perfect for black forest cakes. I never cut corners when it comes to a good vanilla, as you will use less real vanilla to get a remarkable flavor than you could ever get from gallons of a cheap imitation.

vanilla cherries

Yields 6 pints

6 lbs. dark sweet cherries or tart cherries, washed, pits removed

2 cups sugar

2 cups water

½ cup lemon juice

2 Tbsp. vanilla bean paste (or double-strength vanilla)

¼ tsp. salt

¼ tsp. ground cardamom

1. In a large pot, combine the sugar, water, lemon juice, vanilla bean paste, salt, and cardamom. Bring to a rolling boil and reduce to a simmer. Add the cherries to the sugar mixture and heat through. Pack cherries into hot sterilized jars. Ladle hot syrup over the cherries in the jars, allowing ½-inch headspace. Remove the air bubbles. Tighten two-piece cap onto jars.

2. Process in a boiling water-bath for 10 minutes. Transfer to a clean, dry cloth or cooling rack out of the way of any draft. Allow to cool 12 hours before moving jars.

Money-saving tip: Visit a local cherry farm for best prices on cherries. Many local farms will give you a better deal if you pick the cherries yourself. Frozen cherries can be purchased and home canned once defrosted, but be sure to heat them through and follow the full canning directions listed here. Cherry pitting devices are handy tools when canning cherries, and if you'll be doing a lot of cherries over the years, it is a wonderful investment.

I can fix anything with a jar of spiced peaches. You had a bad day at school? I can fix that. You stubbed your toe? I can fix that. Maybe I can't fix a broken toe, but I can make sure my family knows I love them. Spiced peaches are amazing in pie. Try them chopped over waffles or mixed into oatmeal. You'll never be sad again. I promise. Spiced peaches can fix anything. Peaches should be ripe, but not soft or mushy. Look for peaches that are without bruises as well.

spiced peaches

Yields about 6 pints

8 lbs. peaches

1 cup lemon juice

1 cup sugar

4 cups water

2 cups honey

2 Tbsp. ground cinnamon

1 tsp. ground ginger

½ tsp. ground nutmeg

½ tsp. ground allspice

½ tsp. ground clove

¼ tsp. ground cardamom

½ tsp. lemon oil*

1. Wash, drain, and peel peaches. Peaches may be peeled by dropping the whole fruit into a pot of boiling water and letting it blanch for 3–4 minutes. Remove from the boiling water with a large slotted spoon and plunge into an ice water bath. When cool enough to handle, peel off the skin. Remove the pit and scrape out the rough flesh. Coat with lemon juice to keep from browning.

2. In a large pot, combine the sugar, water, honey, cinnamon, ginger, nutmeg, allspice, clove, cardamom, and lemon oil. Simmer until sugar is dissolved. Drain the peaches well. Cook peaches in the pot of sugar syrup, one layer at a time until heated through, about 4 minutes. Sterilize jars. Pack the hot peaches into the jars, leaving ½-inch headspace. Pour the hot syrup over the peaches in the jars, allowing for ½-inch headspace. Remove air bubbles and tighten a two-piece lid onto the jar. Process in a boiling water-bath for 25 minutes. Transfer to a clean, dry cloth or cooling rack out of the way of any draft. Allow to cool 12 hours before moving jars.

Money-saving Tip: Contact your local peach farmers and see if you can pick the fruit yourself. During the seasonal months, peaches are about $1.00 per pound. Most years, when I get the fruit in season the pint jars are about $1.65 per jar. I save even more money if I use jars that I previously purchased. Honey will cost less in bulk, so I split the cost with a friend if we're both making these beautiful peaches.

*Lemon oil can be purchased at gourmet specialty stores and health food stores. This ingredient is optional, but adds remarkable flavor.

Real gourmet poached pears are cooked in a wine syrup with spices and served warm. It depends on the chef, but sometimes they are served on fire! We don't cook with wine at my home, but I've enjoyed this home-canned version using spices and a champagne-flavored candy-oil that adds natural flavor without adding alcohol. Bartlett pears are the best for home canning, even though many use Kieffer pears and other varieties. Make sure the pears are ripe, but not mushy or soft.

poached pears

Yields about 6 pints

8 lbs. Bartlett pears, ripe but not soft

1 cup lemon juice

1 cup sugar

4 cups white grape juice

1 cup honey

2 Tbsp. ground cinnamon

1 tsp. ground ginger

½ tsp. ground nutmeg

½ tsp. ground allspice

½ tsp. ground clove

¼ tsp. ground cardamom

½ tsp. lemon oil*

1 tsp. LorAnn® natural champagne-flavored oil

1. Wash and drain pears. Cut the pears in half and cut out the core. Peel the fruit. Dip in lemon juice to keep from browning. Make a syrup with the sugar, juice, honey, spices, and flavored oils by combining them and cooking over medium heat until sugar dissolves.

2. Drain the pears. Cook the pears in the syrup mixture a few at a time until hot. Pack hot pears in jars, leaving ½-inch headspace. Remove air bubbles. Top with a two-piece canning lid and seal tightly by hand. Process in boiling water-bath for 20 minutes for pints or 25 minutes for quarts.

Money-saving tip: To ensure you don't have any wasted pears, keep them in a cool dry place lower than 70 degrees. They need to be ripe, but not mushy when ready to put in jars.

*Lemon oil is the natural extract of lemon zest (also called an essential oil).

honey cream vanilla oranges

Yields 6 pints

5 lbs. oranges, peeled, supreme sections removed from membrane (about 8 medium)

2 cups water

1¼ cups granulated sugar

1¼ cups liquid honey

3 Tbsp. lemon juice

1 Tbsp. clear double-strength vanilla

① Combine oranges with water to cover in a large stainless steel saucepan. Bring to a boil over medium-high heat. Reduce heat and boil 5 minutes.

② Combine sugar, honey, lemon juice, and vanilla in a clean large stainless steel saucepan. Bring to a boil over medium-high heat, stirring occasionally to dissolve sugar. Add sauce to the oranges in their pot. Bring to a boil. Reduce heat and boil gently until orange slices are well glazed.

③ Gently pack the hot oranges into hot jars using a slotted spoon, leaving ½-inch headspace. Ladle the vanilla syrup into hot jar to cover oranges, leaving ½-inch headspace. Remove air bubbles. Wipe rim. Center lid on jar. Apply band until fit is fingertip tight. Transfer jars to a boiling water-bath canner and process 10 minutes, adjusting for altitude. Remove jars and cool.

Nectarines are perhaps my favorite fruit for a pie. I love using the pecan syrup in the canned version because they lend themselves perfectly to cobblers and to top warm piles of waffles. Nectarines, when prepared, taste similar to a giant cherry. I recommend using Ball® Fruit-Fresh or powdered citric acid to keep the fruit from browning. It is still natural, but you won't have brown jars of fruit.

nectarines in pecan syrup

Yields 4 quarts or 8 pints

8 lbs. nectarines

1 cup sugar

4 cups water

2 cups honey

1½ tsp. whole allspice

1 tsp. LorAnn® natural pecan-flavored oil

Ball® Fruit-Fresh produce protector or powdered citric acid

1. Combine sugar, water honey, spice, and flavor in a half-gallon pot. Bring to a boil; cook until sugar is dissolved. Carefully wash, peel, and pit the fruit. Treat with the Fruit-Fresh according to package directions. Drain nectarines completely. Transfer to sterile jars, keeping the cavity side down, leaving ½-inch headspace. Pour the hot syrup over the nectarines, leaving ½-inch headspace. Remove air bubbles. Wipe rim. Center hot lid on jar. Apply band and adjust until fit is fingertip tight.

2. Process in a boiling water-bath canner for 25 minutes for pints and 30 minutes for quarts, adjusting for altitude. Remove jars and cool.

There are visions of these dancing in my head all year long, not just on the night before Christmas! We use them as the base for cobblers, crisps, and cakes. The addition of a hint of lavender will add a unique and delicate charm to these plums.

sugar plums

Yields 4 quarts or 8 pints

6–10 lbs. plums, whole or halved and pitted (about 60–100 medium)

1½ cups sugar

5¼ cups water

½ tsp. ground ginger

½ tsp. orange oil

1 tsp. lavender petals (optional)

1 Tbsp. vanilla bean paste or double-strength vanilla

① Make syrup by combining sugar, water, ginger, oil, lavender, and vanilla in a half-gallon pot. Bring to a boil over medium-high heat, stirring until sugar is dissolved. Reduce heat to low and keep warm until needed. Do not boil too long or it will thicken.

② Wash plums and drain. Firmly pack plums into sterile jars, leaving ½-inch headspace. Carefully pour hot syrup into hot jars to cover plums, leaving ½-inch headspace. Remove air bubbles and adjust headspace, if necessary, by adding hot syrup. Wipe rim. Center lid on jar. Apply band until fit is fingertip tight. Transfer jars to a boiling water-bath canner 20 minutes for pints and 25 minutes for quarts, adjusting for altitude. Remove jars and cool.

Pineapple upside-down cake will take on a totally remarkable flavor explosion using your own home-canned pineapple. I grill the slices for an extra-caramelized flavor, and it never fails to add an amazing depth to any dish.

grilled pineapple

Yields 4 quarts or 8 pints

12 lbs. pineapple, peeled and cored

2¼ cups sugar

5¼ cups water

½ cup clear white pineapple vinegar (optional, but helps minimize browning)

2 tsp. ground ginger

1 tsp. salt

1. Cut pineapple into ½-inch slices. Grill in a dry grill pan on the stove, or broil in the oven on a metal sheet pan just under the broiling element until caramelized but still firm. About 7 minutes.

2. While grilling pineapple, make a simple syrup with the remaining ingredients. Boil the ingredients in a half-gallon pot on the stove until the sugar is dissolved.

3. Pack hot pineapple into sterilized jars, allowing a ½-inch headspace. Pour the syrup over the pineapple to cover, again making sure there is a ½-inch headspace. Remove all the air bubbles. Tighten a two-piece lid onto the jars.

4. Process in a boiling water-bath for 20 minutes for quarts or 15 minutes for pints. Remove from water. Transfer to a cloth to cool.

Note: Canned pineapple is very susceptible to browning, even when it has been treated with citric acid. I recommend keeping jars in a dark, cool place to minimize browning.

During summer months, the bounty of strawberries is almost too much to bear, especially given the fact that they are so expensive any other time of the year. Stock up! Canning the berries whole can be frustrating when they are too large or mushy. Look for small red-fleshed berries without white flesh or hollow centers. The flavor of strawberries do tend to fade when canned, so the addition of amaretto will greatly enhance these. I like to pack them in smaller jars and use them as Belgian waffle topping.

strawberries amaretto

Yields 6 pints

8 lbs. strawberries, small and firm

1½ cups sugar

1 Tbsp. natural almond-flavored extract

① Wash and drain the berries, removing the cap. Measure berries into a 2-gallon pot. Cover with the sugar and let sit overnight or about 6 hours. Add almond flavor and bring to a low simmer until berries are heated through and sugar is dissolved. Pack into hot sterile jars, leaving ½-inch headspace. Remove air bubbles.

② Add any remaining juice and sugar mixture to the jars from the pot, again being sure to leave ½-inch headspace. Transfer the jars to a boiling water-bath canner. Make sure there are at least 2 inches of water above the jars. Bring water to a rolling boil. Process 10 minutes.

I use adorable little specialty jars for canning these strawberries. They can be purchased online at several different websites. I like jarstore.com.

Pie filling on hand is ready for any occasion. This Christmas Apple-Berry version is delicious!

spiced christmas apple-berry pie filling

Yields 5 quarts

12 cups sliced, peeled, cored apples, treated to prevent browning* and drained (about 12 lbs. medium apples)

2 cups raspberries or blackberries

water

2¾ cups granulated sugar

¾ cup ClearJel® (cooking starch used for preserving)

1 Tbsp. ground Saigon cinnamon

½ tsp. ground nutmeg

½ tsp. ground cardamom

1 tsp. ground ginger

½ tsp. lavender petals (optional)

2½ cups unsweetened apple juice concentrate

1¼ cups cold water

½ cup lemon juice

① Blanch the apple slices, 6 cups at a time, in a large half-gallon pot of boiling water for 2 minutes. Remove with a slotted spoon, fold in the berries, and keep warm in a covered bowl.

② Meanwhile, mix the sugar, ClearJel®, and spices (including optional lavender) in a large stainless steel saucepan. Stir in apple juice and cold water. Bring to a boil over medium-high heat, stirring constantly, and cook until mixture thickens and begins to bubble. Add lemon juice, return to a boil, and boil for 2 minutes, stirring constantly. Drain apple slices and immediately fold into hot mixture, stirring until apples are heated through. Scoop hot apple pie filling into hot jars, leaving 1-inch headspace. Remove air bubbles. Wipe rim. Center lid on jar. Apply band until fit is fingertip tight. Transfer the jars to a boiling water canner for 25 minutes, adjusting for altitude. Remove jars and cool.

*Ball® Fruit-Fresh produce protector or powdered citric acid.

As a kid, I remember drinking Grandma's peach nectar and thinking that I had somehow become part of a secret society of awesomeness! This peach-pineapple nectar is just the right thickness and full of wonderful fruity goodness. I adore mixing it with a natural lemon-lime soda water during hot months for a cool refreshing drink.

peach-pineapple nectar

Yields 6 quarts

3 qts. peeled, sliced peaches

3 cups pineapple juice

1 qt. water

7 cups orange juice

1½ cups honey

½ cup lemon juice

Ⓘ Purée the peaches with the pineapple juice in a good blender until smooth. Transfer to a large 3-gallon nonreactive pot, add all the remaining ingredients, and bring to a boil. Pour the hot nectar into sterile jars, leaving ¼-inch headspace. Process in a boiling water-bath canner for 20 minutes. Remove from water and cool.

Should you have a tree that produces a ton of apples or have the opportunity to make away with an extra bushel or two of tart apples, try making your own fresh apple juice! There is no need to peel the apple when making juice; just remove the stems and chop them. The flavor of fresh apple juice is remarkably light and clean. Strain it through a cheesecloth if you want it to be clear and free of any pulp. This is a bit of a project to make but well worth the effort. This is a spiced variety that I give away at Christmas time with a bow. It is awesome served warm with cookies!

apple spice juice

Yields 6 quarts or 12 pints

24 lbs. apples, stemmed and chopped (about 72 apples)

8 cups water

¼ cup fresh chopped ginger

2 Tbsp. cinnamon

1. Combine the fresh apples, water, and spices in a large saucepan. Bring to a boil. Reduce heat and simmer, stirring occasionally, until apples are tender. Transfer apples and juice, working in batches, to a strainer (making sure that the strainer is lined with several layers of cheesecloth). Let drip, undisturbed, for 2–3 hours. Prepare a boiling water canner. Prepare sterilized canning jars and lids. Simmer the apple juice to 190 degrees F in a large saucepan over medium-high heat.

2. Carefully fill hot jars, leaving ¼-inch headspace. Wipe rim. Center hot lid on jar. Apply band and adjust until fit is fingertip tight. Put jars in the boiling water canner and process for 10 minutes, adjusting for altitude if necessary. Remove jars and cool.

Money-saving tip: Don't buy your apples during the off season, as they will be extremely expensive. Look for local apple farms having "you-pick" events. Make a day of going to the farm with the kids and making not only memories, but also a lot of juice!

Fresh mixed berry juice concentrates are very common these days, but the vast majority of them are a combination of apple juice and a few berries for color. This recipe is pure berry goodness! It will probably cost a lot more than any concentrate if you buy your berries during the winter months. If I am making it from scratch, I wait until summer when the bounty is good and the price is excellent.

mixed berry juice

Yields 4 quarts

3 lbs. blueberries, boysenberries, raspberries (any combination to equal 3 lbs.)

water

1 cup sugar or ½ cup agave nectar

1. Wash berries and crush in a 2-gallon pot over low heat with a small amount of water. Drain juice through a strainer lined with cheesecloth. Measure juice. There should be at least a gallon of juice. Transfer the juice back into a 2-gallon pot, add the sugar or agave nectar, and bring to 190 degrees F. Don't boil it.

2. Fill quart jars, leaving ¼-inch headspace. Tighten two-piece lids to jars and transfer jars to a boiling water-bath canner. Process 15 minutes. Remove from canner and allow to cool completely.

If you have a large harvest of grapes from what you've grown in your garden, juicing is the way to go! Homemade grape juice is crisp and clean-tasting and will be a fast family favorite. Keep in mind that there are several steps. It is usually a two-day project if you want the juice to be clear, as it takes time for the solids to settle on the bottom of the pot.

grape monster

Yields 4 quarts

13 lbs. white or red grapes, stems removed

2 cups water

1 cup sugar (optional)

1. Wash, stem, and drain grapes. Crush grapes in a 2-gallon pot. Add water. Heat grapes for 12 minutes at 190 degrees F. Don't boil them. Strain the juice through cheesecloth into a 2-gallon pitcher. Transfer juice to the fridge and allow to settle 24 hours.

2. Pour juice into another 2-gallon pot, being careful not to disturb the particles settled on the bottom of the pitcher. Add water and sugar. Reheat juice to 190 degrees F. Transfer juice to sterile jars, allowing ¼-inch headspace. Top jars with canning lids tightly. Place jars in a boiling water canner and process 15 minutes. Remove from canner and allow to cool overnight, about 12 hours.

Money-saving tips: Making your own grape juice can cost more money than buying juice premade if you are not getting an amazing price on the grapes. For this reason, I look to local farmers and friends who have a bountiful harvest. You can get a better price on grapes if they are in season.

Pick tomatoes at their peak of freshness and make sure they are from a reputable source. Remove skins by placing tomatoes in a kitchen wire basket that will fit inside a boiling pot of water. Immerse the tomatoes in the boiling water and let them blanch about a minute. Plunge the tomatoes in cold water and the skin should peel off easily.

tomatoes packed with french herbs

Yields 7 half-pints

5 cloves garlic, minced

1 cup white wine vinegar

1¼ cups water

2 Tbsp. sugar

1 tsp. fennel seed

1 Tbsp. dried tarragon

1 Tbsp. dried dill

1 Tbsp. dried oregano

¼ cup good quality balsamic vinegar

9 cups plum tomatoes, peeled, cored, and chopped (about 4 lbs. or 12 medium tomatoes)

1. Mix all ingredients except the tomatoes in a large pot. Bring to a rolling boil and cook 5 minutes. Hand pack the tomatoes into hot jars, leaving ½-inch headspace. Ladle hot vinegar mixture over tomatoes, leaving ½-inch headspace. Remove air bubbles by running a plastic knife along the inside of the jar. Wipe rim. Center hot lid on jar. Apply band and adjust until fit is fingertip tight.

2. Transfer the filled jars in a boiling water canner for 20 minutes, adjusting for altitude. Remove jars and cool completely before moving.

Pick tomatoes at their peak of freshness and make sure they are from a reputable source. For canning, I prefer the flavor of Roma plum tomatoes or heirlooms. However, if you can find any tomatoes that are ripened on the vine before being harvested, they will work. Don't get tomatoes that were picked green and ripened in a warehouse. They will be mealy and are not a taste worth preserving.

whole tomatoes with herbs

Yields 4 pints

6 lbs. tomatoes

water

¼ cup bottled lemon juice

2 tsp. salt

4 tsp. fresh, chopped mixed herbs (rosemary, thyme, and parsley)

1. Get your water canner ready. Heat the jars and lids in simmering (not boiling) water. Set the bands aside for later. Clean the tomatoes. Remove skins by placing tomatoes in a wire basket that will fit inside a boiling pot of water. Immerse the tomatoes in the boiling water and let them blanch about a minute. Plunge the tomatoes in cold water and the skin should peel off easily.

2. Cut off any green areas and remove the core. Leave tomatoes whole or cut into halves or quarters.

3. Place tomatoes in a large saucepan, adding just enough water to keep them covered. Gently boil for about 5 minutes. Prepare hot jar by adding 1 tablespoon lemon juice, ½ teaspoon salt, and 1 teaspoon fresh herbs to each jar. Pack the hot tomatoes into the jars, allowing at least ½-inch headspace. Remove the air bubbles. Add additional boiling water to the jars if needed. Wipe the jar rims with a clean cloth. Apply lids and bands and tighten. Transfer hot jars to a boiling water-bath and process for 35 minutes. Remove from canner and place in a dry place away from any draft. Allow to cool 12–24 hours before moving. Jars should be sealed and the lid should not flex when the center is pressed.

Money-saving tip: I have saved a lot of money on tomatoes by calling local organic farmers and offering to trade my skills as a weed puller/harvester for payment in tomatoes. If you know a farmer who is in need of a few extra hands, you can really save money . . . but you'll have to be willing to work.

whole tomatoes in juice

Yields 6 pints

12 cups halved, cored, peeled tomatoes (about 24 medium or 8 lbs.)
water
spice blend(s), see below
bottled lemon juice
salt (optional)

① Mix tomatoes with just enough water to cover them in a large gallon-sized pot. Boil gently for 5 minutes. To each sterile jar add your chosen spice blend (see below), 1 tablespoon bottled lemon juice, and ¼ teaspoon salt. Loosely pack the tomatoes into your jars, leaving ½-inch headspace. Pour hot cooking liquid over tomatoes, again being sure you are leaving ½-inch headspace.

② Remove air bubbles with a nonreactive tool (like a plastic knife). Wipe rim with a clean cloth. Apply lids and hand tighten. In a water-bath canner, process 40 minutes (adjusting for altitude). Remove jars and cool.

spicy italian spice blend

Yields about 12 pints

1 tsp. basil
2 tsp. thyme
2 tsp. oregano
2 tsp. rosemary
1 tsp. garlic powder
1 tsp. hot pepper flakes

Use 2¼ teaspoons of spice blend to each pint jar.
If omitting hot pepper flakes, use only 2 teaspoons.

mexican spice blend

Yields 12 pints

2 Tbsp. ancho chile powder
1 Tbsp. ground cumin
1 tsp. dry ground oregano
1 Tbsp. garlic powder
1 tsp. ground coriander
1½ tsp. salt

Use 2½ teaspoons of spice blend to each pint jar.

things to know when making homemade tomato sauce

» It usually takes 35 pounds of tomatoes to make a thin sauce to fill 7 quarts. That number goes up to 46 pounds for a thick sauce. It is best to put the acid, salt, and herbs in the jars and then pour in the sauce. This will ensure there is a uniform amount of acid and that the pH level is correct.

» Rather than seasoning the whole sauce, measure the dried herbs into each individual jar. If you choose to use fresh herbs, make sure that you limit the amount to only 1 teaspoon chopped herbs per pint jar. When using fresh herbs, make sure they are unblemished and very clean.

» Prevent the siphon phenomenon: When pressure builds inside home canned jars of tomatoes that are improperly packed, a phenomenon can occur called siphoning. Liquid inside the jar is lost, and this can lead to a lid's failure to seal. Particles from inside the jar get caught between the rim and lid. The danger is greater while processing products with larger volume (like tomatoes and pickles). To prevent this, make sure you're very aware of the headspace guidelines for your products. Make sure you remove as much air as possible in the jar. Don't tightly pack product in jars (firmly pack, but don't cram things in with a lot of force).

» One last word—when processing time is over, it is helpful to turn off the heat, remove the lid of the canner, and wait 5 minutes before removing the jars from the boiling water. Always cool the jars in an upright position. Don't touch them for 24 hours.

tomato sauce with mexican spices

Yields 4 quarts or 8 pints

20 lbs. fresh tomatoes, cored
2 Tbsp. ancho chile powder
2 Tbsp. dry oregano
½ cup bottled lemon juice
salt (optional)
dried oregano and chile powder (optional)

1. Wash tomatoes, carefully removing any bruised or discolored tomatoes. Quarter 6 tomatoes and place in a 2-gallon stainless steel saucepan. Bring to a boil. With a sturdy mashing tool, vigorously crush tomatoes. Stir constantly to release juices. While maintaining heat, add more tomatoes and continue to mash and stir. When all tomatoes have been added, boil, stirring occasionally, until tomatoes are soft and juicy, about 10 minutes.

2. Remove from heat. Press tomatoes through a food mill or Victorio strainer to remove skins and seeds in several batches. Discard skins and seeds. Return mixture to pot. Add the chile powder and dry oregano. Bring to a rolling boil, stirring often. Reduce heat to medium-high and boil until volume is reduced by at least ⅓ for a thin sauce. For a thicker sauce, cook until reduced by half.

3. Before filling each jar with tomato sauce, add lemon juice to the hot jar in the quantity specified below:

   Pint:
   1 Tbsp. bottled lemon juice

   Quart:
   2 Tbsp. bottled lemon juice

4. Scoop the hot tomato sauce into sterile, warm, prepared jars. Leave ½-inch headspace. Remove air bubbles and adjust headspace, if necessary, by adding more sauce. Wipe rim. Apply two-part cap. Screw until fingertip tight. Place jars in canner, ensuring they are completely covered with water. Bring water to a rolling boil and process pint jars for 35 minutes and quart jars for 40 minutes. Wait 5 minutes, remove jars, cool, and store.

tomato sauce with italian herbs and spices

Yields 4 quarts or 8 pints

20 lbs. fresh tomatoes, cored

1 tsp. fennel seed

1 tsp. fresh ground black pepper

2 Tbsp. dry basil

1 Tbsp. dry rosemary

2 Tbsp. dry oregano

½ cup bottled lemon juice

salt (optional)

dried oregano and chile powder (optional)

1. Wash tomatoes, carefully removing any bruised or discolored tomatoes. Quarter 6 tomatoes and place in a 2-gallon stainless steel saucepan. Bring to a boil. With a sturdy mashing tool, vigorously crush tomatoes. Stir constantly to release juices. While maintaining heat, add more tomatoes and continue to mash and stir. When all tomatoes have been added, boil, stirring occasionally, until tomatoes are soft and juicy, about 10 minutes. Remove from heat. Press tomatoes through a food mill or Victorio strainer to remove skins and seeds in several batches. Discard skins and seeds. Return mixture to pot. Add the herbs and spices. Bring to a rolling boil, stirring often. Reduce heat to medium-high and boil until volume is reduced by at least ⅓ for a thin sauce. For a thicker sauce, cook until reduced by half.

2. Before filling each jar with tomato sauce, add lemon juice to the hot jar in the quantity specified below:

   Pint:

   1 Tbsp. bottled lemon juice

   Quart:

   2 Tbsp. bottled lemon juice

3. Scoop the hot tomato sauce into sterile, warm, prepared jars. Leave ½-inch headspace. Remove air bubbles and adjust headspace, if necessary, by adding more sauce. Wipe rim. Apply two-part cap. Screw until fingertip tight. Place jars in canner, ensuring they are completely covered with water. Bring water to a rolling boil and process pint jars for 35 minutes and quart jars for 40 minutes. Wait 5 minutes, remove jars, cool, and store.

spicy tomato juice

Yields 6 quarts or 12 pints

25 lbs. ripe tomatoes, cored (about 75 medium)
2–3 Tbsp. spicy Sriracha sauce*
bottled lemon juice

1. Carefully wash tomatoes and drain. Remove core and blossom ends. Cut tomatoes into quarters. Simmer tomatoes in a large stainless steel saucepan until soft, stirring to prevent sticking. Juice tomatoes in a food processor or food mill. Strain juice to remove peels and seeds. Gently heat the juice 5 minutes at 190 degrees F. Do not boil. Add Sriracha sauce.

2. To each jar add 2 tablespoons bottled lemon juice to each hot quart jar OR 1 tablespoon bottled lemon juice to each hot pint jar. Ladle hot juice into hot jars, leaving ¼-inch headspace. Wipe rim. Top with hot lid and ring. Transfer jars to a boiling water canner, making sure the lids are completely immersed under water. Process 35 minutes for pints and 40 minutes for quarts (always adjust for altitude). Remove jars and cool on a rack or clean cloth.

*Sriracha is a type of hot sauce or chile sauce made from a paste of chile peppers, distilled vinegar, garlic, sugar, and salt.

chapter three

soft spreads

Jams are usually made by taking crushed or puréed fruit and cooking it with sugar until the mixture mounds on a spoon.

tips

» Only make a single batch of jam at a time. Doubling the recipe will not cook correctly and will usually result in the jam not setting correctly.

» Use only top-quality fruit when making jam.

» Usually I combine some very ripe fruit for optimum flavor with some additional fruit that is almost under ripe (not green) to ensure the correct amount of pectin and acid in the spread.

» Always wash fruit and dry well.

» Remove scars or blemishes and don't use fruit that has obvious signs of decay or disease.

» Follow the specific directions for crushing of fruit so that there isn't too much juice expelled into the sauce, as this can inhibit the process.

» My recipes call for sugar, but honey can be used to replace sugar, cup for cup, in the recipes when pectin is used. If you need sugar-free jams, there are low-sugar/no-sugar pectins available. Use the recipes provided by the manufacturer of those products to make sugar-free jams.

» I use extremely potent flavored oils instead of alcohol flavorings in most of my recipes. These were initially designed for candy-making and are available from LorAnn® oils (in most craft stores by the candy-making tools). You may use liquid flavorings, but they tend to cook out and need to be added at the end of cooking time.

» Commercial pectin is used in these recipes. It is a natural product and helps increase the yield of the jam recipes and makes the jam-making process simple.

» Occasionally some jams will develop a layer of foam on the surface during cooking. This is totally normal. This should be removed with a slotted spoon before the jam is transferred to canning jars.

This cherry chipotle jam is amazing on cream cheese bagels. We serve it as an appetizer over cream cheese along with an assortment of crackers. It is also remarkable with baked brie.

low-sugar cherry chipotle jam

Yields 6 half pints

4 cups finely chopped sweet cherries (about 3 lbs.)
1 cup unsweetened white grape juice
1 Tbsp. chipotle peppers* in sauce, chopped fine
3 Tbsp. Ball® RealFruit® Low- or No-Sugar-Needed Pectin

1. Get a boiling water canner ready, as well as jars and lids in simmering water (don't boil). Have rings on hand.

2. In a 2-gallon saucepan, combine cherries, juice, and chipotle peppers. Gradually add the pectin. Bring to a full rolling boil and cook 1 minute. Remove from heat. Carefully remove any foam from the surface of the jam with a slotted spoon. Pour jam into hot jars, allowing ¼-inch headspace. Make sure there are no air bubbles. Wipe the rim with a clean cloth. Top with hot lids and tighten with bands. Transfer to a boiling water canner and process 10 minutes, adjusting for altitude as needed. Remove the hot jars from the water and place on a clean towel to cool.

*Chipotle peppers are fully ripe red jalapeños that have been roasted. They can be found in most Hispanic food sections in major grocery stores and also in specialty gourmet stores.

My grandmother had a giant apricot tree that grew right outside her kitchen door. I remember often as a child climbing into the branches of that tree and eating the fruit while watching the world go by below me. In that same grandma's kitchen, I spent many hours packing apricots into jars and helping mash the fruit for jam. This jam reminds me of her most of all.

grandma's apricot cream vanilla jam

Yields 8 half-pint jelly jars

3 lbs. apricots (weigh after peeling and mashing)

¼ cup lemon juice

7½ cups sugar

1 tsp. vanilla bean paste or double-strength vanilla

¼ tsp. natural Bavarian Cream LorAnn® flavored oil*

¼ tsp. natural Amaretto LorAnn® flavored oil*

¼ tsp. salt

⅛ tsp. fresh grated nutmeg

1 pouch liquid Certo® pectin

1. Get a boiling water canner ready, as well as jars and lids in simmering water (don't boil). Have rings on hand. Combine peeled, mashed apricots in a large 2-quart heavy-bottomed pot. Add lemon juice, sugar, vanilla, flavors, salt, and nutmeg. Bring to a full boil that cannot be stirred down, stirring constantly. Stir in the pectin. Boil hard for 1 minute, stirring constantly. Remove foam if necessary.

2. Ladle hot jam into hot sterile jars, leaving ¼-inch headspace. Remove air bubbles. Wipe rim with a clean cloth. Center hot lid on jar. Apply band and adjust until it is fingertip tight. Process in a boiling water canner for 10 minutes. Remove jars and place on a clean kitchen towel. Allow to cool undisturbed at least 12 hours. Check lids for seal after 24 hours. Lid should not flex up and down when center is pressed. This jam may take about a week to get completely set.

*LorAnn® flavored oils are available at most hobby and craft stores in the cake- and candy-making sections or available on the LorAnn® website. Get the natural varieties whenever possible.

This recipe is ideal if you have a variety of berries on hand but not enough of one single berry to make a batch. I love it most with blackberries and raspberries.

mixed berry bliss jam

Yields 6 half-pint jelly jars

4 cups crushed berries (mix and match your favorites such as strawberries, blueberries, raspberries, and blackberries)

4½ Tbsp. classic pectin

3 cups sugar

1 Tbsp. double-strength vanilla

1. Get a boiling water canner ready, as well as jars and lids in simmering water (don't boil). Have rings on hand. Mix the berries in an 8-quart saucepan. Slowly stir in pectin and stir the mixture to a full rolling boil that cannot be stirred down. Stir constantly. Add all of the sugar and vanilla. Stir until sugar is totally dissolved.

2. Boil hard 1 minute, stirring constantly. Remove from heat. Skim foam if necessary. Scoop the hot jam into hot sterile prepared jars, leaving ¼-inch headspace. Wipe rims. Apply lids. Tighten. Transfer the filled jars in a boiling water-bath canner, ensuring jars are covered by 1–2 inches of water. Process jars for 10 minutes, always adjusting for altitude. Turn off heat, remove lid, and let jars stand for 5 minutes.

3. Remove jars and cool. After 24 hours, check the seal. The lid should not flex at all when pressed in the center of the lid.

I receive letters from all over the world asking me for recipes and ideas. A letter that I will never forget came from Gabbi in South Africa asking me how to make fresh fig jam. It took me a while to find fresh figs here where I live, but once I did, I could never go back to dried figs for jam ever again! Look for them in season at local specialty stores or find a friend with a fig tree! I bet they'll give you some for free! Figs are amazing. They all have a skin. I love the black variety. The fruit is mild and slightly tart and is much like a bland kiwi.

south african–inspired fresh fig jam

Yields 7 half-pints

2 lbs. black figs (4 cups), washed and chopped

½ cup lemon or lime juice

7 cups sugar

1 box sure-gel fruit pectin

1½ tsp. vanilla

1½ tsp. ground cinnamon

a dash of ground nutmeg and cardamom

1. Get a boiling water canner ready, as well as jars and lids in simmering water (don't boil). Have rings on hand. Heat the figs and lemon juice in a large pot on the stove until soft, about 10 minutes. Mash or run the figs through a blender. I used a blender or a food mill. If you peeled the figs, the blending step isn't necessary. You can just mash the fruit. Make sure you mash it very well, as I've noticed it helps the jam hold thick better when the fruit is very well mashed. I like keeping the skin. It makes the jam red colored and I like the flavor.

2. Return the fruit purée to the pot. Add the sugar and gel. I also add 1½ teaspoons vanilla, 1½ teaspoons ground cinnamon, a dash of nutmeg, and ground cardamom. Simmer for 20 minutes until thick. Transfer hot jam to clean and sterilized canning jars with new lids. Put canning jars in a hot water-bath canner on the stove, making sure the water is well over the lids. Bring water to a boil. Process 10 minutes. Remove from the water-bath and put on a clean towel. Do not disturb jars for 12 hours. This will ensure a good seal.

spiced blueberry–amaretto jam

Yield 6 half-pints

2½ pints ripe blueberries

1 Tbsp. lemon juice

¼ tsp. ground nutmeg

1 tsp. high-grade cinnamon (or Chef Tess Wise Woman of The East Spice Blend)

¾ cup water

1 box (1¾ ounces) powdered pectin

5½ cups sugar

1 tsp. almond extract

① Get a boiling water canner ready, as well as jars and lids in simmering water (don't boil). Have rings on hand. Wash and thoroughly crush blueberries, one layer at a time, in a saucepan (or, for smoother jam, purée in a food processor). Add lemon juice, spices, and water. Stir in pectin and bring to a full, rolling boil over high heat, stirring frequently.

② Add the sugar and return to a full rolling boil. Boil hard for 1 minute, stirring constantly. Remove from heat and stir in almond extract. Quickly skim off foam and fill hot sterile jars, leaving ½-inch headspace. Wipe jar rims. Adjust lids and process for 10 minutes in boiling water-bath.

kiwi tropical twist jam

Yield 4 half pint jelly jars

2 cups kiwifruit, peeled and crushed (about 5 medium)

⅔ cup crushed pineapple

⅓ cup lime juice

3 cups sugar

¼ tsp. natural rum LorAnn® flavored oil

6 Tbsp. Ball® Real Fruit™ Classic Pectin

1. Get a boiling water canner ready, as well as jars and lids in simmering water (don't boil). Have rings on hand. In a large saucepan, combine all ingredients except the pectin. Bring to a boil over high heat, stirring often. Boil hard 5 minutes. Slowly stir in the pectin and boil constantly 1 minute more. Remove from heat.

2. Carefully remove any foam from the surface of the jam with a slotted spoon. Pour jam into hot jars, allowing ¼-inch headspace. Make sure there are not any air bubbles. Wipe the rim with a clean cloth. Top with hot lids and tighten with bands. Transfer to a boiling water canner and process 10 minutes, adjusting for altitude as needed. Remove the hot jars from the water and place on a clean towel to cool. Check the seal after 24 hours.

If there's any of this remarkable stuff left in the jam pan after I fill the mason jars, I shame-lessly dunk my head in there and lick it off the bottom of the pan. Okay . . . maybe I don't. That would get mango jam junk in my hair and then I would look crazy. (Yes. Only then would I look crazy.) This jam is incredible on a bagel with cream cheese. It is amazing on ribs and grilled chicken. I've used it over baked brie. It is by far my favorite topping for a cracker.

mango jalapeño jam

Yields 8 half pints

2 lbs. mangoes (after peeling and pitting)

4 jalapeños, seeded and minced

¾ cup lemon juice

7½ cups sugar

1 tsp. salt

2 pouches liquid pectin

① Get a boiling water canner ready and place jars and lids in simmering water (don't boil). Have rings on hand. Mash mangoes over low heat in a 1-gallon heavy-bottomed pot.

② Add all of the remaining ingredients except the pectin. Boil 5 minutes. Add pectin and boil 1 minute longer. Put in sterile canning jars (makes 8 1-cup jars). Seal lids.

③ Process cans in boiling water for 10 minutes if at sea level. Remove cans from the canner and place on dry kitchen towel.

④ Allow to cool for 12 hours. Check the seals. If properly sealed, store for up to a year. If it didn't seal, it may be refrigerated for up to 2 months.

Note: I use kitchen gloves when I seed and cut jalapeños . . . because I tried it without them once and made the mistake of rubbing my eye. It was not a mistake I ever want to repeat. I'm sure it was hilarious to watch.

black forest jam

Yields 7 half pints

4 cups sugar

⅓ cup sifted cocoa powder

3½ cups cherries, pitted and chopped (about 3 lbs. fresh or frozen)

2 Tbsp. lemon juice

2 (3-oz.) pouches Ball® RealFruit™ liquid pectin

⅓ cup unsweetened flaked coconut

½ tsp. natural cherry-flavored LorAnn® oil

¼ tsp. natural rum-flavored LorAnn® oil

① Get a boiling water canner ready, as well as jars and lids in simmering water (don't boil). Have rings on hand. Mix the sugar and cocoa powder in a bowl. In a large saucepan, mix the cherries, lemon juice, and sugar/cocoa blend. Bring mixture to a rolling boil. Stir in the pectin and boil 1 minute more, stirring well. Remove the pan from the heat and add the remaining ingredients. Carefully remove any foam from the jam with a slotted spoon.

② Pour jam into hot jars, allowing ¼-inch headspace. Make sure there are no air bubbles. Wipe the rim with a clean cloth. Top with hot lids and tighten with bands. Transfer to a boiling water canner and process 10 minutes, always adjusting for altitude as needed. Remove the hot jars from the water and place on a clean towel to cool. Check the seal after 24 hours.

What if you could have all the flavors of apple pie and cherry pie mashed together in a spreadable concoction that could be smeared on toast? Would you do it? We love this jam! It is wonderful between layers of cake and on pancakes as well. I prefer the liquid pectin in this recipe because you will get a higher yield on how many jars the recipe will make.

cherry apple pie jam

yields 6 half-pint jars

5½ cups applesauce

1½ cups chopped fresh plums

1 cup dried cherries, chopped

¾ cup water

¼ cup lemon juice

1 tsp. ground cinnamon

¼ tsp. ground allspice

⅛ tsp. butternut natural-flavored LorAnn® oil

1 tsp. vanilla bean paste or double-strength vanilla

4 cups granulated sugar, measured into separate bowls

½ cup firmly packed light brown sugar

1 pouch liquid pectin

① Get a boiling water canner ready, as well as jars and lids in simmering water (don't boil). Have rings on hand. Measure 5½ cups applesauce, plums, and dried cherries into a 6- or 8-quart sauce pot. Stir in water, lemon juice, cinnamon, allspice, flavored oils, and vanilla. Bring mixture to full rolling boil on high heat, stirring constantly. Stir in sugars.

② Return to full rolling boil and boil 5 minutes, stirring constantly. Stir in liquid pectin and boil for 1 minute. Remove from heat. Skim off any foam with metal spoon. Ladle immediately into prepared jars, allowing ¼-inch headspace. Wipe jar rims and threads. Cover with lids. Screw bands tightly. Transfer jars to boiling water-bath canner and process 10 minutes. Remove jars and place upright on a towel or rack to cool completely.

There is a story behind this jam. I have never been to Paris, but for many years I promised myself that I'd come up with a spread that I could put in my French macarons that would mimic all the smells of Paris at Christmas. I think it is perfect.

christmas in paris jam

Yields 8 half-pints

2 cups purée of fresh plum

1 cup applesauce

½ cup chopped cherries

½ cup peeled and chopped peaches

2 cups sugar

1½ cups brown sugar

1 Tbsp. minced fresh ginger

1 tsp. anise seed

1 tsp. lavender petals*

1 tsp. rose petals*

1 tsp. cinnamon

⅛ tsp. nutmeg

⅛ tsp. ground cardamom

2 tsp. double-strength vanilla

1　Get a boiling water canner ready, as well as jars and lids in simmering water (don't boil). Have rings on hand. In a 1-gallon heavy-bottomed pot, pour 1 cup of the sugar. Heat over low heat without liquid until the sugar starts to brown and melt but not burn. Add the fruit and remaining sugars. Cook over a low simmer for 20–25 minutes.

2　Add the remaining ingredients and stir well. Ladle into sterile jars, allowing ¼-inch headspace. Wipe rims with a clean cloth and apply lids and bands until finger tight. Transfer to a boiling water canner and process 10 minutes, adjusting as necessary for altitude. Remove jars and cool. Check the seal on the jars after 24 hours to be sure all sealed correctly. Lid shouldn't flex when the middle is pressed with a firm finger.

*Culinary-grade flowers must be purchased from a spice company, as the dry flowers in most craft stores are treated with chemicals that are potentially dangerous. Find a friend who grows the flowers if you cannot find them. They are also available online from San Francisco Spice Company.

This is the nonalcoholic version of a strawberry margarita in a jam vortex of flavor. Enjoy it on a shortcake with fresh whipped cream.

strawberry margarita jam

Yields 5 half-pints

6 cups strawberries, halved and hulled (about 3½ 1-lb. containers)

2 cups prepared applesauce

¼ cup lemon juice

4 cups granulated sugar

1 package of classic pectin

½ tsp. orange brandy natural-flavored LorAnn® oil

½ tsp. strawberry natural-flavored LorAnn® oil

1. Get a boiling water canner ready, as well as jars and lids in simmering water (don't boil). Have rings on hand. In a large gallon-sized heavy pot, combine the strawberries, applesauce, and lemon juice. Bring to a boil and mash fruit. Add sugar, lower heat to medium, and continue cooking and stirring for 10 minutes, until sugar is dissolved. Add pectin and flavors. Bring to a hard boil for 1 minute.

2. Remove from the heat and gently remove any foam with a slotted spoon. Pour the hot jam into jars, allowing ¼-inch headspace. Wipe rims with a clean cloth and apply lids and bands until finger tight. Transfer to a boiling water canner and process 10 minutes, adjusting as necessary for altitude. Remove jars and cool. Check the seal on the jars after 24 hours to be sure all sealed correctly. Lid shouldn't flex when the middle is pressed with a firm finger.

Different from a jam, a conserve usually contains a small amount of nuts and dry fruit. This is one of my favorite combinations using blueberry and pecan. Make sure when you're giving this spread away as gifts that the recipient doesn't have a nut allergy.

mom's blueberry lemon pecan supreme conserve

Yields 4 half-pints

2½ pints ripe blueberries

¼ cup lemon juice

5½ cups sugar

¾ cup water

½ cup golden raisins

1 box (1¾ ounces) powdered pectin

½ cup fine minced pecans

¼ tsp. lemon oil

½ tsp. LorAnn® natural butter pecan flavor oil

1. Wash and thoroughly crush blueberries, one layer at a time, in a saucepan. Add lemon juice, sugar, water, and raisins. Stir in pectin and bring to a full, rolling boil over high heat, stirring frequently. Boil hard for 1 minute, stirring constantly.

2. Remove from heat and stir in nuts and oils. Quickly skim off any foam. Fill hot sterile jars, leaving ½-inch headspace. Wipe jar rims. Adjust lids and process for 10 minutes in boiling water-bath.

fruit butters

Fruit butter is made by cooking the pulp of fruits to a thick spread. Generally, spices are added to the spread mixture. They are cooked long enough to round up on a spoon. Remember to prepare all spreads in a single batch, as they will always set up better, and doubling the batches may keep the final product from gelling.

Apple butter has been the most popular fruit butter for many generations and is a classic spread on toasted bread. I use the best quality cinnamon and vanilla I can find, as it will take less of those ingredients to produce a wonderful rich flavor in the apple butter.

apple spice butter
Yields 3 pints

4 pounds tart green apples, peeled and chopped

1 cup lemon juice

1 cup orange juice

4 cups sugar

1 Tbsp. Saigon cinnamon

¼ tsp. ground clove

½ tsp. ground ginger

1 Tbsp. vanilla bean paste or double-strength vanilla

1. Mix the apples and juices in a large 1-gallon saucepan. Bring to a boil. Reduce heat and simmer until apples begin to soften. Purée mixture in a food processor. Measure 8 cups of apple pulp.

2. Combine the apple pulp with the remaining ingredients and simmer until thick enough to round up on a spoon. Stir frequently. Scoop the hot apple butter into sterilized jars, allowing ¼-inch headspace. Make sure to remove air bubbles. Top with hot lids and tighten. Transfer to boiling water-bath canner. Process 10 minutes. Remove from canner and allow to cool in a draft-free area.

Apple butter can be made quickly using prepared applesauce. This is a great way to cut the preparation time in half while still maximizing the flavor.

simple spiced apple berry butter

Yields 3 pints

8 cups prepared or canned applesauce

$\frac{1}{2}$ cup fresh or frozen raspberries

4 cups sugar

$\frac{1}{2}$ cup fresh lemon juice

2 tsp. ground cinnamon

1 tsp. ground cloves

$\frac{1}{4}$ cup chopped candied ginger

$\frac{1}{2}$ tsp. nutmeg

$\frac{1}{4}$ tsp. lavender, crushed fine

1 bay leaf

1 Tbsp. vanilla extract

1 Combine all ingredients in a heavy 4-quart pot and simmer 15–20 minutes until very thick. Remove bay leaf. Pour boiling hot apple butter in hot jars (clean and sterilized!), leaving ¼-inch headspace. Wipe rim and place lids and rings. Water-bath in boiling water for 10 minutes for both pints and quarts.

The addition of natural maple flavor in this apricot butter makes it especially delicious on breakfast pastries and in between layers of spiced French toast.

maple apricot butter

Yields 3 pints

24 medium apricots (about 2 pounds)

water

3 cups sugar

2 Tbsp. lemon juice

½ tsp. nutmeg

1 tsp. cinnamon

2 Tbsp. finely chopped, candied ginger

½ tsp. LorAnn® natural maple-flavored oil

1 tsp. almond extract

① Wash apricots. Pit and halve. Combine apricots with ½ cup water in a pan. Simmer until apricots are soft. Purée using a food mill but don't liquefy. Measure 1½ quarts apricot pulp. Combine apricot pulp and sugar in a large pot.

② Cook until thick enough to round up on a spoon. As it thickens, stir frequently to prevent sticking. Add the remaining ingredients. Stir well. Ladle hot butter in pint jars, leaving ¼-inch headspace. Remove bubbles, wipe rim, and place lids and rings. Process in water-bath for 10 minutes.

Nothing says "fall" like the combination of apple and spiced cranberry, and this fruit butter is perfect for those cold autumn mornings when nothing but a warm muffin with a slather of spiced tart-sweet spread will satisfy.

apple-cran vanilla butter

Yields 3 pints

2 quarts applesauce (8 cups)

½ cup dry cranberries, chopped fine

4 cups sugar

½ cup fresh lemon juice

2 tsp. ground cinnamon

1 tsp. ground cloves

¼ cup chopped candied ginger

½ tsp. nutmeg

¼ tsp. lavender, crushed fine

1 bay leaf

1 Tbsp. vanilla extract

① Combine all ingredients in a heavy 4-quart pot and simmer 15–20 minutes until very thick. Remove bay leaf. Pour boiling hot butter in hot sterilized jars, leaving ¼-inch headspace. Wipe rim and place lids and rings. Process in a water-bath canner for 10 minutes.

My photographer, Laura, said that the mere mention of spiced peach butter was enough to make her husband swoon. Let the swooning commence. You've got the recipe for love right here, baby!

spiced peach butter

Yields 4 pints

2 lbs. peaches, peeled, halved, and pitted (about 24 medium)

½ cup water

3 cups granulated sugar

½ cup fresh lemon juice

2 tsp. ground cinnamon

1 tsp. ground cloves

¼ cup chopped candied ginger

½ tsp. nutmeg

¼ tsp. lavender, crushed fine

1 bay leaf

2 tsp. butter pecan LorAnn® natural-flavored oil

1 Tbsp. vanilla extract

① Combine the peaches and water in a large stainless steel saucepan. Bring to a boil over medium-high heat. Reduce heat and boil gently, stirring occasionally, until peaches are soft, about 20 minutes. Purée mixture in a food mill or a food processor fitted with a metal blade, working in batches, and purée just until a uniform texture is achieved. Do not liquefy. Measure 6 cups of purée.

② Mix the purée and sugar in a clean large stainless steel saucepan. Stir until sugar dissolves. Bring to a boil over medium-high heat, stirring frequently. Reduce heat and boil gently, stirring frequently, until mixture thickens and holds its shape on a spoon. Stir in lemon juice and spices. Carefully pour the hot butter into hot jars, leaving ¼-inch headspace. Remove air bubbles. Wipe rim. Apply canning lid and band until fit is fingertip tight. Transfer the hot jars into a boiling water canner for 10 minutes, adjusting for altitude. Remove jars and cool.

A hint of champagne mingled with the warmth and richness of spiced ginger is followed by a lingering subtle kiss of lavender and vanilla bean in this sweet poached pear butter. It is a complex and artistic spread that will keep you coming back for more.

poached pear butter

Yields 4 pints

2 qt. pears, peeled and chopped (8 cups)

4 cups sugar

1 cup white grape juice concentrate (defrosted)

1 tsp. LorAnn® champagne-flavored oil

2 tsp. ground cinnamon

1 tsp. ground cloves

¼ cup chopped candied ginger

½ tsp. nutmeg

¼ tsp. lavender, crushed fine

1 bay leaf

1 Tbsp. vanilla extract

① Combine all ingredients in a heavy 4-quart pot and simmer 15–20 minutes until very thick. Remove bay leaf. Pour boiling hot butter in hot jars (clean and sterilized!). Leave ¼-inch headspace. Wipe rim and place lids and rings. Water-bath in boiling water for 10 minutes for both pints and quarts.

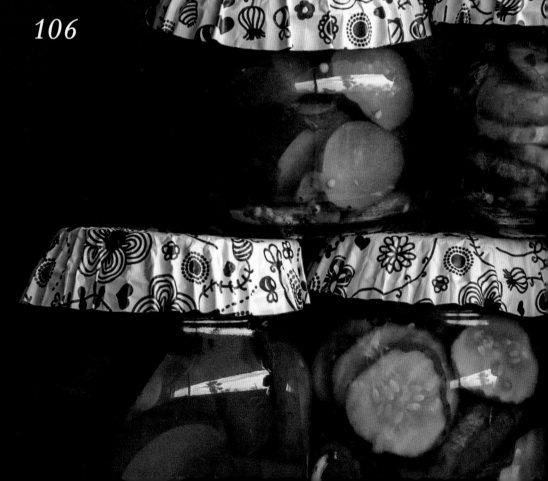

chapter four

pickled foods

pickling success begins with a few simple tricks

» Use fresh cucumbers. If the cucumbers have been sitting around longer than a few days, the natural enzyme action will have already begun to break down the natural pectin in the cucumber. If you cannot pickle the cucumbers shortly after they are harvested, putting them in refrigeration is the best tool for keeping the enzyme activity at a minimum. Once they are soft because of enzyme activity, they cannot be made crisp again.

» Pick cucumbers that are less than 2 inches in diameter. They will always make crisper pickles.

» Avoid using cucumbers that have been waxed, as these will not allow the brine to come through.

» Don't use burpless cucumbers, as they produce an enzyme that will soften pickles, and their skin is thick, making it harder to brine.

» The use of alum is no longer recommended for crisp pickles.

» I do recommend using a calcium chloride product on the market called Pickle Crisp®. This product provides the calcium to help firm pectin of the cucumbers. Follow the manufacturer's directions on the jar.

» One of the simplest methods of firming pickles is to use ice. Soak cucumbers or other vegetables in ice water or layer with crushed ice for 4 to 5 hours before pickling. Sometimes this step is combined with a salt solution.

» Do not pack cucumbers too tightly in the jar. Leave ample room for the pickling solution.

» Always use vinegar that has at least a 5% acidity. Vinegars will list this on their labels.

» Always process jars in a boiling water-bath the full amount of time in the recipe.

» Use scientifically proven recipes. Don't alter the amount of vinegar or vegetables in the recipe.

I was raised with peanut butter–dill pickle sandwiches. That might explain how weird I am. I was raised by a pickle-slinging kitchen wizard. No arguments. These dill pickles are pure magic and a family classic recipe (even for the weirdest families).

basic dill darlings

Yields 7 pints or 3 quarts

8 lbs. small pickling cucumbers, cut lengthwise into halves

1 cup sugar

½ cup pickling salt

1 qt. white vinegar

4 cups water

¼ cup pickling spice mix

7 sprigs fresh dill

7 cloves garlic

Ball® Pickle Crisp (optional)

1. Completely wash cucumbers and drain well. In a large saucepan, mix the sugar, salt, vinegar, and water. Tie the spice mixture in a cheesecloth bag tightly. Add the spice bag to the sugar-vinegar mixture. Simmer 20 minutes. Remove the spice bag. Meanwhile, pack the drained cucumbers in the hot jars, leaving ½-inch headspace.

2. Slip a sprig of fresh dill and a clove of garlic into each jar, as well as the Pickle Crisp (as directed on package). Pour the hot spice vinegar mixture over the cucumbers. Remove air bubbles, again allowing ½-inch headspace. Fix lids to jars. Transfer sealed jars to a boiling water canner and process 15 minutes.

I have a cabinet at my house that my children do not dare open. It is the sweet-hot cabinet. There is always a bottle of these in the fridge just for me. My kids think they're too hot. I don't make them for the kids. For a grown-up, they're just hot enough and sweet-crispy with some perfect spice. Sometimes, if I really love someone, I'll even share. Then again, don't count on me sharing. You better make your own.

sweet-hot pickles

yields 4 pints

6 cups thin-sliced cucumbers (use Kirby or small unwaxed cucumbers)

½ lb. jalapeños, sliced thin (stems removed)

water

ice

¼ cup salt

2 cups sugar

2 Tbsp. minced garlic

½ tsp. curry powder

¼ tsp. ground clove

2 Tbsp. mustard seed

2 tsp. celery seed

2 cups cider vinegar (5% acid)

Ball® Pickle Crisp (optional)

① Slice cucumbers and jalapeños thin and place in a large bowl with salt. Cover with water and some ice. Leave out at room temperature for 3 hours.

② In a large pot, combine the sugar, garlic, curry, cloves, mustard seed, celery seed, and vinegar. Bring slowly to a boil and boil for 5 minutes. Drain the vegetables in a colander and rinse them well with cold water. Add them to the hot syrup and heat just below boiling. Spoon into hot sterilized jars, fill with the cooking syrup and the Pickle Crisp (as directed on package), leaving ¼-inch headspace.

③ Run a non-metal knife along the edge of the jar to remove excess air. Seal with hot lids. Tighten canning lid. Place in boiling water-bath canner and wait for water to return to a boil. Process 10 minutes. Remove and place on a clean kitchen towel in a place free from drafts. Allow to cool 12 hours undisturbed.

Sweet pickles are not something I crave very often, unless they're tiny little nibbles like a baby gherkin. What is it about the baby size that make them so adorable? I'm not sure, but that size makes them perfect for pickling! Look for the baby ones at special farmer's markets or grow your own.

sweet baby gherkins

Yields 6 half-pint jars

6 cups mini gherkin cucumbers
¼ cup salt
water
ice
2 cups sugar
2 Tbsp. minced garlic
½ tsp. curry powder
¼ tsp. ground clove
1 Tbsp. mustard seed
1 tsp. celery seed
2 cups cider vinegar (5% acid)
Ball® Pickle Crisp (optional)

1. Place cucumbers in a large bowl with salt. Cover with water and some ice. Leave out at room temperature for 6 hours.

2. In a large pot, combine the sugar, garlic, curry, cloves, mustard seed, celery seed, and vinegar. Bring slowly to a boil and boil for 5 minutes. Drain the cucumbers in a colander and rinse them well with cold water. Add them to the hot syrup and heat just below boiling. Spoon into hot sterilized jars and fill with the cooking syrup and the Pickle Crisp (as directed on package), leaving ¼-inch headspace.

3. Run a non-metal knife along the edge of the jar to remove excess air. Seal with hot lids. Tighten canning lid. Place in boiling water-bath canner and wait for water to return to a boil. Process 10 minutes. When time is finished, remove and place on a clean kitchen towel in a place free from drafts. Allow to cool 12 hours undisturbed.

The first time I ever tried pickled cauliflower I thought I had died and gone to heaven. It was tart and hot with the perfect amount of sweetness and spice. Now we have to have a bottle of this mix at all times in the fridge. I slip into the kitchen late at night when nobody is awake and can frequently be found with my fingers in the cauliflower jar. Don't judge me. They're a vegetable. It is a healthy addiction. They are the perfect addition to pasta salads and relish trays, and I personally can't have potato salad without a cup or two of this cauliflower chopped into the dressing. It is awesome!

pickled cauliflower–n–garden power

Yields about 5 pints

10 cups cauliflowerets

1 cup sliced carrots (about ¼-inch thick)

1 cup thin-sliced cucumbers

1 cup sliced red bell pepper

¼ cup pickling salt

2 cups sugar

1 Tbsp. mustard seed

1 Tbsp. dill seed

1½ tsp. celery seed

4 cups distilled vinegar (5% acidity)

1½ tsp. hot red pepper flakes

Ball® Pickle Crisp (optional)

1. Mix vegetables and salt in a clean sink or gallon-sized container. Cover the vegetables with ice and salt and allow to sit 2–3 hours. Drain and rinse with cool water. In a large saucepan, combine sugar, mustard, dill seed, celery seed, vinegar, and pepper flakes. Bring to a boil. Add vegetables and heat to 190 degrees F. Reduce heat and simmer 5 minutes.

2. Transfer vegetable mixture to sterile jars and cover with liquid and the Pickle Crisp (as directed on package), leaving ½-inch headspace. Remove air bubbles. Fix two-piece canning lid and hand tighten. Transfer to a boiling water-bath canner and process 10 minutes.

First off, I have to say that, before I was married, I was not a fan of bread and butter pickles. Had anyone mentioned they wanted to make a bread and butter pickle, I would have said that I had no idea how to even start. When we first got married and Ace put a jar of bread and butter pickles in the shopping cart, I remember thinking perhaps he wasn't my soul mate. It turns out that in a good marriage we only need to agree on the things that are our core principles . . . and be okay with each other having preferences that may not matter. Pickles would be a matter of preference. Bread and butter pickles have grown on me over the years, and now I love them on smoky ham sandwiches with perky fresh tomatoes.

my bread and butter pickles

yields 4 pints

6 cups thin-sliced cucumbers (use Kirby or small unwaxed cucumbers)
1 pound white onion, cut thin
¼ cup salt
2 cups sugar
2 Tbsp. minced garlic
½ tsp. curry powder
¼ tsp. ground clove
1 Tbsp. mustard seed
1 tsp. celery seed
2 cups cider vinegar 5% acid
Ball® Pickle Crisp (optional)

(1) Slice cucumbers and onions thin and place in a large bowl with salt. Cover with water and some ice. Leave out at room temperature for 3 hours.

(2) In a large pot, combine the sugar, curry, cloves, mustard seed, celery seed, and vinegar. Bring slowly to a boil and boil for 5 minutes. Drain the vegetables in a colander and rinse them well with cold water. Add them to the hot syrup and heat just below boiling. Spoon into hot sterilized jars and fill with the cooking syrup and the Pickle Crisp (as directed on package), leaving ¼-inch headspace.

(3) Run a non-metal knife along the edge of the jar to remove excess air. Seal with hot lids. Tighten canning lid. Place in boiling water-bath canner and wait for water to return to a boil. Process 10 minutes. Remove and place on a clean kitchen towel in a place free from drafts. Allow to cool 12 hours undisturbed.

BUTTER

plant #49-34   sweet cream   net wt 4oz (113g)

We call my mother-in-law Cussing Granny on my food blog. I don't know why. She doesn't cuss. She was raised on a farm in Colorado. They cooked on a wood stove and made everything from scratch. Her grandma used to make the best corn relish. I personally had never heard of such a thing as corn relish until Cussing Granny mentioned it being her favorite topping for fried eggs. How country can that be? Fried eggs with corn relish screams "I'm a country bumpkin." So, I set out trying to find it. It wasn't in any of our local stores that I could see. I scoured cookbooks and finally found a recipe in the Fannie Farmer Cookbook by Marion Cunningham. It used eighteen ears of fresh corn and a lot of other veggies . . . and it took forever to chop everything. However, I rolled up my sleeves and decided to give it a whirl. When it was done, it was tart and sweet and hot and heavenly. I wanted it in My Sloppy Joes and my tuna salad. I found great uses for a sweet hot corn relish. The recipe below is adapted a bit using my own variation of the spices.

sweet and hot corn relish

yields 11 pints

18 ears of sweet corn, husked and with corn kernels sliced off (15 cups)

4 cups minced sweet Vidalia onion

2 cups chopped bell pepper

1 cup chopped green or red hot peppers, seeds removed

½ cup shredded carrots

½ cup chopped fresh parsley

8 cups vinegar

3 cups sugar

1 Tbsp. celery seed

2 Tbsp. mustard seed

2 tsp. curry powder

2 Tbsp. salt

2 tsp. red pepper flakes

① Combine all ingredients in a 3-gallon pot and boil 1 hour until thick. Fill sterilized hot pint jars with relish, leaving ¼-inch headspace. Top with new lids that have been sterilized. Seal with a ring. Process in a boiling water-bath canner for 15 minutes. Remove from boiling water and place on a clean kitchen towel or cooling rack. Allow to cool away from any draft 12 hours. Check seals.

Money-saving tip: If you are trying to save time or money, it may be a good option for you to buy frozen corn that has been cut off the ear. Look at the bag to determine how many cups are in the frozen package. Defrost and use as you would regular corn in this recipe.

True confession: I cannot eat grilled hamburgers without a good dill relish. I don't know why, but it's the truth. That being said, this is not only a good dill relish, but a classy, delicious dill relish. Can relish be classy? You're about to find out!

classy dill-icious relish

Yields 7 pints

8 lbs. pickling cucumbers

½ cup pickling or canning salt

2 tsp. ground turmeric

4 cups water

2½ cups finely chopped onions

2 Tbsp. dill seeds

2 Tbsp. ready-to-use chopped garlic

4 cups white vinegar

1. In a food processor fitted with a metal blade or a food grinder, working in batches, finely chop the cucumbers. Transfer batches to a glass or stainless steel bowl as they are completed. Sprinkle with pickling salt and turmeric. Add water, cover, and let stand in a cool place (70–75 degrees) for 3 hours. Transfer to a colander placed over a sink and drain thoroughly. Rinse with cool water and drain thoroughly again. Using your hands, squeeze out excess liquid.

2. Meanwhile, prepare canner, jars, and lids. In a large stainless steel saucepan, combine drained cucumbers, onion, dill seed, garlic, and vinegar. Bring to a boil over medium-high heat. Reduce heat and boil gently, stirring occasionally, until slightly thickened and vegetables are heated through, about 10 minutes. Ladle hot relish into hot jars, leaving ½-inch headspace.

3. Remove air bubbles and adjust headspace, if necessary, by adding hot relish. Wipe rim. Center lid on jar. Screw band down until resistance is met, then increase to finger tight. Place jars in canner, ensuring they are completely covered with water. Bring to a boil and process for 15 minutes. Wait 5 minutes, then remove jars, cool, and store.

Grilled onion relish is the best companion to braised meats, pot roast, and grilled salmon. My family loves it drizzled over cream cheese and served with crackers.

peppery grilled onion relish
Yields 6 pints

1 Tbsp. vegetable oil

1½ cups red onion, chopped

8 cups sweet yellow bell peppers, chopped

8 cups red bell peppers, chopped

3 hot red peppers, minced fine

1 tsp. mustard seed

1 tsp. ground coriander

½ tsp. allspice

½ tsp. thyme

1 Tbsp. black pepper

1¾ cups sugar

2 Tbsp. salt

3½ cups vinegar

1. Heat a large 12-inch skillet to the smoking point with 1 tablespoon of vegetable oil. Add the red onions to the pan and do not stir. Grill onions until browned. Remove from the heat. Combine the remaining vegetables in a large bowl, covering them with boiling water. Let them sit 10 minutes. Drain. Cover again with boiling water. Sit another 10 minutes. Drain. Combine spices, sugar, salt, and vinegar in a gallon-sized pot. Simmer the spice mixture for 15 minutes.

2. Add the drained vegetables and the onions to the spice mixture. Bring to a boil. Transfer relish to the sterilized jars, being sure to leave ½-inch headspace. Remove any air bubbles. Tightly seal with canning lid. Transfer to boiling water-bath and process 15 minutes. Remove from canner and allow to cool.

Here it is. There has to be sweet pickle relish. Granny can't make potato salad without it. My kids can't eat hotdogs without it. Half my family in Utah can't eat French fries without it mixed with the ketchup and mayo for fry sauce. Therefore, there must be sweet pickle relish. My recipe logic is undeniable.

sweet baby boy pickle relish

Yields 7 pints

8 lbs. pickling cucumbers

½ cup pickling or canning salt

2 tsp. ground turmeric

4 cups water

2½ cups finely chopped onions

2 cups sugar

2 Tbsp. dill seeds

2 Tbsp. ready-to-use chopped garlic

4 cups white vinegar

1. In a food processor fitted with a metal blade or a food grinder, working in batches, finely chop the cucumbers. Transfer batches to a glass or stainless steel bowl as they are completed. Sprinkle with pickling salt and turmeric. Add water, cover, and let stand in a cool place (70–75 degrees) for 2 hours. Transfer to a colander placed over a sink and drain thoroughly. Rinse with cool water and drain thoroughly again. Using your hands, squeeze out excess liquid.

2. Meanwhile, prepare canner, jars, and lids. In a large stainless steel saucepan, combine drained cucumbers, onion, sugar, dill seed, garlic, and vinegar. Bring to a boil over medium-high heat. Reduce heat and boil gently, stirring occasionally, until slightly thickened and vegetables are heated through, about 10 minutes. Ladle hot relish into hot jars, leaving ½-inch headspace. Remove air bubbles and adjust headspace, if necessary, by adding hot relish. Wipe rim. Center lid on jar. Screw band down until resistance is met, then increase to finger tight. Place jars in canner, ensuring they are completely covered with water. Bring to a boil and process for 15 minutes. Remove canner lid. Wait 5 minutes, then remove jars, cool, and store.

I cannot eat a fresh tomato sandwich without a thick slathering of this red bell pepper relish on the bread. I think it completes the flavor and fills my heart with songs of joy. It is an outstanding burst of flavor and color garnish to any grilled chicken or roasted vegetable. Plus, it makes itself particularly useful in enhancing the flavor of any Italian salad dressing.

smoky red bell pepper relish

Yields 6 half-pint jars

6 red bell peppers, chopped

1½ cups red onions, minced

1 cup balsamic vinegar

½ cup sugar (or honey)

1 Tbsp. salt

½ tsp. celery seed

¼ cup minced garlic

1 tsp. ground fennel seed

⅛ tsp. liquid smoke flavor

1. Mix all ingredients in a large pot and simmer 30 minutes. Spoon into clean hot jars and fill with the cooking liquid, leaving ⅛-inch headspace. Seal. Process in boiling water-bath canner for 10 minutes.

Tomato relish is a sweet, tangy sauce used to bring succulence and bold flavor to your roasted meats, grilled mushrooms, and roasted summer squash. Use a good balsamic vinegar that will give a deep rich color to the sauce, and don't be afraid of how much garlic the recipe calls for in the preparation. It will mellow when cooked.

sassy mom's tomato relish

Yields 8 half-pint jars

6 cups peeled, chopped tomatoes

1½ cups red onions, minced

1 cup balsamic vinegar

½ cup sugar (or honey)

1 Tbsp. salt

½ tsp. celery seed

¼ cup minced garlic

1 tsp. ground fennel seed

Mix all ingredients in a large pot and simmer 30 minutes. Spoon into clean hot jars, fill with the cooking liquid, leaving ⅛-inch headspace, and seal. Process in boiling water-bath canner for 10 minutes.

chapter five

low-acid foods

pressure canning basics

Many people process their own meat or vegetables for longer-term shelf life. It is recommended that home-canned meat be used within a year of being processed. As I'm liable, I'm not going to ever suggest that it could be safe for very much longer than that. Sorry, folks. The only meats I suggest for really long shelf life (10–15 years) are freeze-dried meats. The moisture content is the key. If food is stored in liquid, there's always going to be a possibility for bacteria growth. The most deadly canning concerns happen with low-acid foods, and those botulism spores can only be killed at the higher temperatures that pressure canners produce. Boiling water canners top out at 212 degrees F at sea level (botulism needs to be heated to 240 degrees F to be killed).   I am often asked how to do this and how to do it in such a way that it doesn't cause food-borne illness. Pressure canning is the answer. This is the method of canning used for low-acid foods like meat, vegetables, and some fruits (depending on their pH levels).

Some reasons for processing your own meat and vegetables:

» Save money and buy when meat or vegetables are on sale

» Convenient cooked meals on hand for easy use

» Processing game and wild animal meat (or home-raised animals)

» Preserving vegetables for use from the garden or local farmer's markets

» Preparing for any emergency

Pressure canning is done in a large pressure cooker specifically designed for home canning. It is not okay to use a regular pressure cooker for home canning unless specified by the manufacture to be safe for this method! It is, however, okay to use a pressure canner for large batches of pressure-cooked foods. Please make sure if you are home canning meat that you have a home canner that has been approved for home canning safely. Also, I'm a food-safety freak. I will always give you the best possible safety information for your family that I have.

pressure processing procedure

(1)   Carefully place canning rack in the bottom of the pressure canner and fill water level to 2 inches (or whatever your model of canner specifies). Heat to a simmering 180 degrees and hold the temperature and water level.

(2)   Follow recipe preparations and fill jars as directed, carefully measuring headspace and using the air-removing tool to release any air inside the jar. Top with sterilized jar lids and rings. Tighten the rings.

(3)   Place jars on rack inside of the pressure canner. Lock lid in place according to your canner's specifications. Leave the weight off the top vent or open the petcock. At this point, set your stove to medium-high heat until the steam just flows in an even stream from the vent pipe or petcock. Exhaust the steam from the canner for 10 solid minutes.

(4)   Place the weight on the vent or close the petcock. If you've done it correctly, the canner should reach pressure in 5 minutes or less. When the gauge reaches the pressure you need, start your timer and adjust the heat on your stove to medium-high or whatever temperature is necessary to maintain the pressure for the whole processing time.

(5)   When the time is up, turn off your heat and remove the canner from the heat. Allow it to cool naturally (that means don't remove the weight or do anything). Just let it sit there until the pressure is at zero. Let it cool an additional 10 minutes, then remove the lid. Unlock the lid and let the steam escape. Wait another 10 minutes and then remove the jars.

(6)   Take the jars from the canner and place upright on a dry towel, cooling rack, or cutting board, allowing 1–2 inches of wiggle-space between each jar (for air circulation). DON'T tighten the bands when they are still warm! Jars may burst if you do so! Cool in an area free from any draft for 12–14 hours.

prevent the siphoning phenomenon

To prevent siphoning of products from inside the jars into the pressure canner, monitor the pressure closely during processing, making only gradual adjustments to the heat level. Allow the pressure canner to cool completely and naturally before releasing the lid. Once the lid is removed, let the jars cool inside the pressure canner for a further 10 minutes. In either case, when removing jars, be sure to lift them straight up, without tilting, and cool them upright, undisturbed, for 24 hours.

Candied carrots are a side dish that we served often at the restaurant I first worked in following culinary school. I had no idea at the time that I could mimic that flavor in a home-canned product. I love these! The kiss of sugar and pepper is just the perfect addition.

candied carrots

Yields 4 pints

4 lbs. carrots (1-inch diameter)

2 tsp. salt

¼ cup sugar or honey

1 tsp. crushed red peppers (optional)

① Wash and drain the carrots. Peel and wash again. Slice carrots. Pack into hot jars, leaving 1-inch headspace. Add ½ teaspoon salt, 1 tablespoon sugar, and ¼ teaspoon pepper to each jar. Pour boiling water over carrots, again leaving 1-inch headspace. Remove air bubbles. Hand-tighten two-piece lids onto jars. Process pints in pressure canner 25 minutes at 10 pounds of pressure at sea level. Adjust for altitude.

② When the time is up, turn off your heat and remove the canner from the heat. Allow it to cool naturally (that means don't remove the weight or do anything). Just let it sit there until the pressure is at zero. Let it cool an additional 10 minutes, then remove the lid. Unlock the lid and let the steam escape. Wait another 10 minutes and then remove the jars.

③ Take the jars from the canner and place upright on a dry towel, cooling rack, or cutting board, allowing 1–2 inches of wiggle-space between each jar (for air circulation). DON'T tighten the bands when they are still warm! Jars may burst if you do so! Cool in an area free from any draft for 12–14 hours.

If you're not a fan of beets, then no amount of dill in the world will make them taste good to you. However, I've been raised with fresh beets from the garden, and I adore a good clean dirt taste. Just kidding. Actually, when done right, there will not be a hint of dirt flavor, but just the peppery taste of a good red beet.

dilled beets

Yields 4 pints

4 lbs. beets (1-inch diameter)

2 tsp. salt

1 Tbsp. plus 1 tsp. dry dill weed

1 tsp. crushed red peppers (optional)

1. Wash and drain the beets. Peel and wash again. Slice beets. Pack into hot jars, leaving 1-inch head-space. Add ½ teaspoon salt, 1 teaspoon dill, and ¼ teaspoon pepper to each jar. Pour boiling water over beets, again leaving 1-inch headspace. Remove air bubbles. Hand-tighten two-piece lids onto jars. Process pints in pressure canner for 30 minutes at 10 pounds of pressure at sea level. Adjust for altitude.

2. When the time is up, turn off your heat and remove the canner from the heat. Allow it to cool naturally (that means don't remove the weight or do anything); just let it sit there until the pressure is at zero. Let it cool an additional 10 minutes, then remove the lid.

3. Unlock the lid, let the steam escape. Wait another 10 minutes and then remove the jars. Take the jars from the canner and place upright on a dry towel, cooling rack, or cutting board, allowing 1–2 inches of wiggle-space between each jar (for air circulation). DON'T tighten the bands when they are still warm! Jars may burst if you do so! Cool in an area free from any draft for 12–14 hours.

cream-style corn with chiles

Yields 4 pints

12 lbs. corn in husks (about 4 ears) per pint jar

water

2 tsp. salt (optional)

2 tsp. crushed red pepper

1 tsp. ground cumin seed

(1) Shuck the corn, remove the silk, and wash the cobs. Place the corn in a large pot of boiling water for 5 minutes. Drain the corn and let it cool slightly. Cut the corn off of the cob and, with a spoon, scrape the cob to expel pulp and corn milk. Measure the corn, pulp, and milk together. You should add 1 cup of boiling water to every 2 cups of pulp mixture you have. Carefully transfer the pulp/water mixture to a large gallon-sized pot and simmer 6 minutes until very hot. Spoon the corn and liquid mixture into hot sterile jars. Leave 1-inch headspace. To each jar add ½ teaspoon salt, ½ teaspoon crushed red pepper, and ¼ teaspoon ground cumin. Remove any air bubbles. Wipe the rim with a clean cloth and tighten the two-piece lid and band onto the jars until fingertip tight.

(2) Transfer jars to a pressure canner. Process 1 hour and 25 minutes for pints, adjusting for altitude. When the time is up, turn off your heat and remove the canner from the heat. Allow it to cool naturally (that means don't remove the weight or do anything); just let it sit there until the pressure is at zero. Let it cool an additional 10 minutes, then remove the lid. Unlock the lid and let the steam escape. Wait another 10 minutes and then remove the jars.

(3) Take the jars from the canner and place upright on a dry towel, cooling rack, or cutting board, allowing 1–2 inches of wiggle-space between each jar (for air circulation). DON'T tighten the bands when they are still warm! Jars may burst if you do so! Cool in an area free from any draft for 12–14 hours.

whole kernel corn with black pepper

Yields 2 quarts or 4 pints

water

12 lbs. corn on the cob

2 tsp. salt

2 tsp. fresh cracked pepper

1. Bring a half-gallon of water to a boil while you husk the corn and remove the silk. Remove the kernels from the cob and pack the corn loosely in hot prepared sterile jars, allowing 1-inch headspace. Don't press the kernels down, just pack them loosely. Add ½ teaspoon salt and pepper to the pint jars OR 1 teaspoon salt and pepper to the quart jars. Pour boiling water over the corn, allowing 1-inch headspace. Remove any air bubbles. Tighten the two-piece lid and band onto the jar, fingertip tight.

2. Transfer to pressure cooker and process pints for 55 minutes and quarts for 1 hour 25 minutes at 10 pounds of pressure at sea level, always adjusting for altitude as needed.

3. When the time is up, turn off your heat and remove the canner from the heat. Allow it to cool naturally (that means don't remove the weight or do anything); just let it sit there until the pressure is at zero. Let it cool an additional 10 minutes, then remove the lid. Unlock the lid and let the steam escape. Wait another 10 minutes and then remove the jars.

4. Take the jars from the canner and place upright on a dry towel, cooling rack, or cutting board, allowing 1–2 inches of wiggle-space between each jar (for air circulation). DON'T tighten the bands when they are still warm! Jars may burst if you do so! Cool in an area free from any draft for 12–14 hours.

Money-saving tip: I wait for the few weeks when corn is incredibly cheap at the grocery stores and farmer's markets. The sweet, fresh corn is amazing when home canned. If you'll be processing a lot of corn, it is a good idea to get a corn cob cleaning tool. The work is cut in half. If nothing else, make sure you have a super sharp knife!

Never can mushrooms that you have not purchased from a reputable source. It usually takes one pound of mushrooms per half-pint of canned mushrooms, as they shrink during cooking. Canning mushrooms will save money in the long run, especially given how quickly mushrooms tend to get moldy in the fridge. Make sure you use small mushrooms that are cut in half or left whole to your preference. Mushrooms are only recommended to be canned in half-pint or pint jars.

marinated mushrooms

Yields 4 half-pints

4 lbs. small mushrooms
1 tsp. salt (optional)
2 tsp. Italian herbs, dry
¼ cup golden balsamic vinegar
water

1. Completely clean the dirt from mushrooms using a soft brush. Rinse well under cool water. Remove stem ends, leaving small mushrooms intact or cut in half. In a large saucepan, cover mushrooms with water. Boil 5 minutes. Pack the mushrooms in hot jars, allowing 1-inch headspace. Add ¼ teaspoon salt, ½ teaspoon Italian herbs, and 1 tablespoon balsamic vinegar to each jar.

2. Pour boiling water over mushrooms, again only leaving 1-inch headspace. Remove any air bubbles and apply the lid and band. Process half-pints 45 minutes at 10 pounds pressure, adjusting pressure as needed for altitude.

3. When the time is up, turn off your heat and remove the canner from the heat. Allow it to cool naturally (that means don't remove the weight or do anything); just let it sit there until the pressure is at zero. Let it cool an additional 10 minutes, then remove the lid.

4. Unlock the lid and let the steam escape. Wait another 10 minutes and then remove the jars. Take the jars from the canner and place upright on a dry towel, cooling rack, or cutting board, allowing 1–2 inches of wiggle-space between each jar (for air circulation). DON'T tighten the bands when they are still warm! Jars may burst if you do so! Cool in an area free from any draft for 12–14 hours.

mixed vegetable medley

Yields 7 quarts or 14 pints

7 cups sliced carrots, 1-inch diameter and ¼-inch thick

7 cups carrots

7 cups green beans, cut in 2-inch pieces

6 cups zucchini, chopped

1 cup sweet red bell pepper, diced

½ cup all-purpose seasoning blend (optional)

① Prepare pressure canner. Prepare jars and rings according to manufacturer's instructions, keeping the jars and lids simmering (not boiling). In a 3-gallon pot, combine vegetables and cover with water. Boil at least 5 minutes Pack the hot vegetables and liquid into sterile quart jars. Add 1½ teaspoons of seasoning in pint jars or 1 tablespoon all-purpose seasoning in quart jars (optional).

② Allow 1-inch headspace on each jar. Remove any air bubbles and top with lid and tighten ring. Transfer jars to the hot pressure canner. Process 1 hour 15 minutes for pint OR 1 hour 30 minutes for quarts.

③ When the time is up, turn off your heat and remove the canner from the heat. Allow it to cool naturally (that means don't remove the weight or do anything); just let it sit there until the pressure is at zero. Let it cool an additional 10 minutes, then remove the lid. Unlock the lid to let the steam escape. Wait another 10 minutes and then remove the jars.

④ Take the jars from the canner and place upright on a dry towel, cooling rack, or cutting board, allowing 1–2 inches of wiggle-space between each jar (for air circulation). DON'T tighten the bands when they are still warm! Jars may burst if you do so! Cool in an area free from any draft for 12–14 hours.

buttery irish potatoes

Yields 4 pints

4 lbs. white potatoes, peeled, cubed in 1-inch chunks

water

2 tsp. salt (optional)

2 tsp. granulated garlic

2 tsp. granulated onion

1. Prepare a pressure canner. Prepare jars and lids, keeping the jars and lids in simmering water (not boiling) until ready to use. Set rings aside.

2. Cover potatoes with water in a 2-gallon or larger stock pot. Boil at least 10 minutes. Pack the hot potatoes into jars, allowing 1-inch headspace. Add ½ teaspoon salt, garlic, and onion to each jar. Pour boiling water over the potatoes in the jars. Remove any air bubbles. Tighten lid and ring onto the jars. Transfer jars to pressure canner and process 35 minutes at 10 pounds of pressure, adjusting as necessary for altitude. When the time is up, turn off your heat and remove the canner from the heat. Allow it to cool naturally (that means don't remove the weight or do anything); just let it sit there until the pressure is at zero. Let it cool an additional 10 minutes, then remove the lid. Unlock the lid to let the steam escape. Wait another 10 minutes and then remove the jars.

3. Take the jars from the canner and place upright on a dry towel, cooling rack, or cutting board, allowing 1–2 inches of wiggle-space between each jar (for air circulation). DON'T tighten the bands when they are still warm! Jars may burst if you do so! Cool in an area free from any draft for 12–14 hours.

These are absolutely the best topping ever for hamburgers and a wonderful way to preserve a bounty of beautiful, bold onions.

sweet red onions

Yields 8 pints

5 qt. thick-sliced red onions (about 30 large)

2 Tbsp. salt

2 cups honey

3 cups water

1 cup grape juice or white wine

2 Tbsp. thyme, dry

1 Tbsp. celery seed

1. Prepare a pressure canner. Prepare jars and lids, keeping the jars and lids in simmering water (not boiling) until ready to use. Set rings aside.

2. Place onions in a sterilized sink or divided between two large bowls. Sprinkle with salt. In a large saucepan, simmer the honey, water, juice, thyme, and celery seed. Cook over low heat and reduce the sauce by half, cooking about 25 minutes. Stir often to prevent scorching. Pack the onions into prepared jars, allowing 1-inch headspace. Pour the hot sauce over the onion, again allowing 1-inch headspace and removing any air bubbles. Tighten lid and ring onto the bottles. Transfer the jars to a pressure canner. Process 15 minutes.

3. When the time is up, turn off your heat and remove the canner from the heat. Allow it to cool naturally (that means don't remove the weight or do anything); just let it sit there until the pressure is at zero. Let it cool an additional 10 minutes, then remove the lid. Unlock the lid to let the steam escape. Wait another 10 minutes and then remove the jars. Take the jars from the canner and place upright on a dry towel, cooling rack, or cutting board, allowing 1–2 inches of wiggle-space between each jar (for air circulation). DON'T tighten the bands when they are still warm! Jars may burst if you do so! Cool in an area free from any draft for 12–14 hours.

Some sweet potatoes are packed in a slimy syrup that overwhelms the flavor of the potatoes. These are not those sweet potatoes. Packed with a hint of brown sugar and just the right amount of spice, these are going to be a fast favorite side dish for any feast!

spiced sweet potatoes

Yields 4 pints

4 lbs. sweet potatoes, peeled and diced

2 tsp. cinnamon

1 tsp. ginger

½ cup brown sugar

water (boiling)

1. Prepare a pressure canner. Prepare jars and lids, keeping the jars and lids in simmering water (not boiling) until ready to use. Set rings aside.

2. In a 2-gallon pot, cover peeled, cut potatoes with water and boil 10 minutes. In each jar add 2 tablespoons brown sugar, ½ teaspoon cinnamon, and ¼ teaspoon ginger. Pack the hot sweet potatoes into the jars, allowing 1-inch headspace. Pour boiling water into the jar, removing any air bubbles and again allowing 1-inch headspace. Adjust lid and ring.

3. Transfer jars to a pressure canner and process 1 hour 5 minutes at 10 pounds of pressure, adjusting as needed for altitude. When the time is up, turn off your heat and remove the canner from the heat. Allow it to cool naturally (that means don't remove the weight or do anything); just let it sit there until the pressure is at zero. Let it cool an additional 10 minutes, then remove the lid. Unlock the lid to let the steam escape. Wait another 10 minutes and then remove the jars.

4. Take the jars from the canner and place upright on a dry towel, cooling rack, or cutting board, allowing 1–2 inches of wiggle-space between each jar (for air circulation). DON'T tighten the bands when they are still warm! Jars may burst if you do so! Cool in an area free from any draft for 12–14 hours.

meat under pressure

Meat, poultry, and fish are low-acid foods and must be processed using a pressure canner for optimal safety. Use the tested processing times that have been provided in this book and other sources, along with the recommendation for the pounds-per-square-inch that a weight will provide for each kind of meat.

General guidelines for canning meat or poultry:

» Can only good quality meats.

» If you are raising your own meat, chill it to 40 degrees F or below soon after slaughter. This will prevent spoilage.

» Keep all meat clean. Rinse chicken and turkey in cold water and drain.

» Freeze meat and store frozen if it is being held more than a few days before canning.

» Always thaw previously frozen meat in the fridge at 40 degrees F or lower until the majority of the ice has disappeared. Larger cuts of meat could take several days to defrost, but it is the safest method.

» Trim gristle and fat off meat before canning. Too much fat left on meat can rise to the top of the jar and interfere with the jar's sealing process.

Note: Individuals using a weighted-gauge canner at altitudes less than 1000 feet may use 10 PSI instead of 15 PSI for the canner pressure. This will improve nutrient and quality retention. Check with your local county extension office or Soil Conservation District for altitude information. For more information about food safety, call USDA's Meat and Poultry Hotline at 1-800-535-4555.

Safety note: Home pressure-canned food is good up to a year after processing, if kept in a cool, dry place. Label each jar clearly with the date of production so there aren't any questions as to how long the food has been around the house. If the bottles ever start to ooze, mold, or bubble on the shelf . . . they're evil and need to be destroyed! Be safe. If obvious signs of spoilage are clear, don't open the jars. Dispose of them. Don't feed them to your pets. Now that you know the safety instructions, remember that by following a few rules, you can make meals that are actually delicious and safe at home!

how much meat will I need?
it doesn't say in your recipes!

Preparing meat during the home canning process is the only section of this book where there are not exact yields for jars. Instead, there are basic directions. The number of jars you make is only limited by the amount of kitchen space you have.

For safety reasons, please remember it is not recommended to ever thicken any of the broth for home canning meat before it is processed.

Precooking breakfast sausage and packing in patties is a convenient way to have cooked meat on hand for making into any breakfast skillet or hash. Be sure to avoid seasoning with sage, as it becomes bitter during the canning process.

breakfast sausage

It usually takes about 1 pound of meat to fill a pint jar. Do not pack ground meat raw.

(1) Use fresh ground pork or turkey and season with salt, pepper, cayenne, thyme, rosemary, and basil as desired. Shape the sausage into patties or links that are 3–4 inches long. Transfer to a heavy skillet and brown. Drain off fat and pack into hot jars, allowing 1-inch headspace in the jars. Pour hot broth or stock over sausage, again allowing 1-inch headspace. Purge of any air bubbles.

(2) Top with hot lids and tighten bands onto jars. Transfer jars to pressure canner and process at 10 pounds pressure for 1 hour 15 minutes for pints and 1 hour 30 minutes for quarts. Only start the timer when the pressure canner is up to temperature and pressure.

(3) When time is over, turn off the heat and allow the pressure cooker to decompress naturally. Do not run under water or remove the weight until the gauge reads "0" and the weight doesn't hiss when touched. That would be a sure sign that it needs more time to cool. Remove jars and cool in a draft-free area. Do not disturb them! Check lids for seal after 24 hours. Lid should not flex up and down when center is pressed. At this point, remove the rings. Wash and sanitize the outsides of the jars with warm soapy water.

You may prefer to pack your pork unseasoned with only a teaspoon of salt per jar and use it to taste. My family just prefers having it ready to shred for tacos, as that is where we use it most often. It takes approximately 1 pound of meat to fill a pint jar and 2 pounds per quart jar.

southwestern sweet-hot pork tenderloin

Mix the sweet-hot seasoning:

2 Tbsp. ancho chile powder

1 Tbsp. garlic powder

1 Tbsp. onion powder

2 Tbsp. salt

1 Tbsp. ground cumin

1 tsp. citric acid

1 Tbsp. lemon zest, dry

¼ cup sugar

boiling water or beef broth on hand to fill in the spaces of the jars

1. Slice the raw pork loin into 1-inch slices and season generously with sweet-hot seasoning. Pack meat into prepared, sterile, hot jars, allowing 1-inch headspace. Pour hot water or broth over tenderloin, removing air bubbles. Top with hot lid and tighten ring. Transfer jars to pressure canner and process pints for 1 hour 15 minutes or quarts for 1 hour 30 minutes at 10 pounds of pressure, adjusting as needed for altitude.

2. Only start the timer when the pressure canner is up to temperature and pressure. When time is over, turn off the heat and allow the pressure cooker to decompress naturally. Do not run under water or remove the weight until the gauge reads "0" and the weight doesn't hiss when touched. That would be a sure sign that it needs more time to cool. Remove jars and cool in a draft-free area. Do not disturb them! Check lids for seal after 24 hours. Lid should not flex up and down when center is pressed. At this point, remove the rings. Wash and sanitize the outsides of the jars with warm soapy water.

This can be used for beef, lamb, pork, veal, or venison. It will take approximately 1 pound of roast to fill a pint jar and 2 pounds per quart. If you prefer to season meat with just salt, it will take 1 teaspoon of salt per quart. Browning the pot roast before you pack it in jars means you won't have jars of gray meat lining you pantry. Nobody wants to eat gray meat, ever.

balsamic peppercorn pot roast

Prepare peppercorn glaze by combining:

1 cup balsamic vinegar

1 cup honey

½ cup Worcestershire sauce

2 Tbsp. minced rosemary

2 Tbsp. cracked black pepper

2 Tbsp. minced garlic

boiling water or beef broth on hand to fill the spaces of the jars

1. Cut the meat into jar-length strips that are ½-inch to 1-inch thick. In a roasting pan, brown roast in an oven at 350 degrees F, usually 30 minutes per pound. Coat the meat with a generous coating of the peppercorn glaze, usually ½ cup of glaze per pound.

2. Cook meat until well browned but not cooked through. Pack the hot meat into prepared, sterile, hot canning jars, allowing 1-inch headspace. Pour hot broth over the meat, again allowing 1-inch headspace. Remove any air bubbles. Top the jars with hot lids and tighten with band to fingertip tight. Transfer jars to a prepared pressure canner and process 1 hour 15 minutes for pints or 1 hour 30 minutes for quarts. Only start the timer when the pressure canner is up to temperature and pressure.

3. When time is over, turn off the heat and allow the pressure cooker to decompress naturally. Do not run under water or remove the weight until the gauge reads "0" and the weight doesn't hiss when touched. That would be a sure sign that it needs more time to cool. Remove jars and cool in a draft-free area. Do not disturb them! Check lids for seal after 24 hours. Lid should not flex up and down when center is pressed. At this point, remove the rings. Wash and sanitize the outsides of the jars with warm soapy water.

This is another recipe that will work with beef, veal, lamb, pork, or venison. Herbs are optional, and doing the plain, unseasoned meat is always a choice. We like adding herbs and garlic just because it adds so much flavor. Be sure to brown the meat and double the ingredients for quart jars.

garlic and herb stew meat

1 lb. chunked stew meat per pint

½ tsp. salt per pint

1 tsp. granulated garlic per pint

1 tsp. mix of equal parts rosemary and oregano

1. Get the pressure canner ready. Heat and sanitize jars. Keep lids and jars in simmering water and ready to use. Don't boil lids. Keep bands on hand.

2. Carefully cut the meat into chunks. Roast the meat in a hot oven at 425 degrees F for 20–25 minutes until browned but not overcooked. Prepare broth for the meat or heat a pot of boiling water.

3. Fill the jars with hot meat, leaving 1-inch headspace. Add 1 teaspoon salt to each quart jar or ½ teaspoon to each pint jar, if desired. For garlic and herb variation, add 1 teaspoon granulated garlic and 1 teaspoon dry herbs of your choice to the meat as well.

4. Pour the prepared hot broth over the meat, again leaving 1-inch of headspace. Purge any air bubbles from the jar. Wipe the rim with a clean cloth. Fit the lid and band on the jar and tighten. Transfer jars to pressure canner and process at 10 pounds of pressure 1 hour 15 minutes for pints and 1 hour 30 minutes for quarts. Always adjust for changes in altitude as needed. Start the timer when the pressure canner is up to temperature and pressure.

5. When time is over, turn off the heat and allow the pressure cooker to decompress naturally. Do not run under water or remove the weight until the gauge reads "0" and the weight doesn't hiss when touched. That would be a sure sign that it needs more time to cool. Remove jars and cool in a draft-free area. Do not disturb them! Check lids for seal after 24 hours. Lid should not flex up and down when center is pressed. At this point, remove the rings. Wash and sanitize the outsides of the jars with warm soapy water.

Probably the most practical of all home-canned meats to have on hand is chicken. It is simply one of the most versatile to use in almost any recipe calling for chicken. I prefer to pack my chicken boneless and skinless. Make sure your working conditions are well sanitized and that you work in batches small enough to fill your canner without jars of the uncooked product sitting for more than a few minutes before being processed.

basic chicken

chicken, boneless and skinless (usually 1 lb. for pints, 2 lbs. for quarts)
salt (½ tsp. for pints, 1 tsp. for quarts)
water or chicken broth, boiling

① Get the pressure canner ready. Heat and sanitize jars. Keep lids and jars in simmering water and ready to use. Don't boil lids. Keep bands on hand. Raw pack the chicken into hot jars, allowing 1-inch headspace. Add 1 teaspoon salt to each quart jar, ½ teaspoon to each pint jar. Pour the prepared hot broth over the meat, again leaving 1-inch headspace. Purge any air bubbles from the jar. Wipe the rim with a clean cloth. Fit the lid and band on the jar and tighten.

② Transfer jars to pressure canner and process at 10 pounds of pressure 1 hour 15 minutes for pints and 1 hour 30 minutes for quarts. Always adjust for changes in altitude as needed. Start the timer when the pressure canner is up to temperature and pressure. When time is over, turn off the heat and allow the pressure cooker to decompress naturally. Do not run under water or remove the weight until the gauge reads "0" and the weight doesn't hiss when touched. That would be a sure sign that it needs more time to cool.

③ Remove jars and cool in a draft-free area. Do not disturb them! Check lids for seal after 24 hours. Lid should not flex up and down when center is pressed. At this point, remove the rings. Wash and sanitize the outsides of the jars with warm soapy water.

Purchase a few extra turkeys when the price goes way down for the holidays. Turkey can be used any time of the year. If you have the freezer space, wait until after the hustle and bustle of the holidays to can it.

basic turkey

turkey meat, boneless and skinless (usually 1 lb. for pints, 2 lbs. for quarts)
salt (½ tsp. for pints, 1 tsp. for quarts)
water or chicken broth, boiling

1. Get the pressure canner ready. Heat and sanitize jars. Keep lids and jars in simmering water and ready to use. Don't boil lids. Keep bands on hand. Raw pack the turkey into hot jars, allowing 1-inch headspace. Add 1 teaspoon salt to each quart jar, ½ teaspoon to each pint jar. Pour the prepared hot broth over the meat, again leaving 1 inch of headspace. Purge any air bubbles from the jar. Wipe the rim with a clean cloth. Fit the lid and band on the jar and tighten.

2. Transfer jars to pressure canner and process, at 10 pounds of pressure, 1 hour 15 minutes for pints and 1 hour 30 minutes for quarts. Always adjust for changes in altitude as needed. Start the timer when the pressure canner is up to temperature and pressure.

3. When time is over, turn off the heat and allow the pressure cooker to decompress naturally. Do not run under water or remove the weight until the gauge reads "0" and the weight doesn't hiss when touched. That would be a sure sign that it needs more time to cool. Remove jars and cool in a draft-free area. Do not disturb them! Check lids for seal after 24 hours. Lid should not flex up and down when center is pressed. At this point, remove the rings. Wash and sanitize the outsides of the jars with warm soapy water.

I've said it for years: soup is way overpriced in the grocery store. It's mostly vegetables and water and those are things I can get for screaming deals if I shop carefully. That being said, we have had a lot of vegetable soup over the years. It is super healthy to eat and so delicious!

classic vegetable soup

Yields 14 pints or 7 quarts

8 cups tomatoes, peeled and diced (about 12 large)

6 cups potatoes, peeled and diced (about 6 medium)

6 cups carrots, peeled and diced (about 12 medium)

4 cups peas, fresh or frozen, defrosted

4 cups corn, whole kernel, uncooked

1 cup celery, chopped (about 2 stalks)

1 cup bell pepper, diced fine (about 2 peppers)

1½ cups onion, chopped (about 2 medium)

¼ cup garlic, minced

¼ cup parsley, minced

6 cups vegetable stock or water

1 Tbsp. salt

1 Tbsp. pepper

1½ tsp. thyme

1½ tsp. cumin

1. Combine all ingredients in a 3-gallon pot and simmer 15–20 minutes. Prepare pressure canner and jars, keeping jars and lids in simmering (not boiling) water. Keep bands on hand. Scoop prepared soup into jars, allowing 1-inch headspace. Remove any air bubbles and top with lid. Tighten band onto jar and transfer jars to pressure canner. Process pints for 55 minutes and quarts for 1 hour 25 minutes at 10 pounds pressure, always adjusting for altitude as needed. Start the timer when the pressure canner is up to temperature and pressure.

2. When time is over, turn off the heat and allow the pressure cooker to decompress naturally. Do not run under water or remove the weight until the gauge reads "0" and the weight doesn't hiss when touched. That would be a sure sign that it needs more time to cool. Remove jars and cool in a draft-free area. Do not disturb them! Check lids for seal after 24 hours. Lid should not flex up and down when center is pressed. At this point, remove the rings. Wash and sanitize the outsides of the jars with warm soapy water.

The key to really great stew is caramelizing the meat and onions well enough that the flavor goes deep. Take the extra few minutes to do this right, and people will be begging for your stew!

mountain man beef stew

Yields 3 quarts or 7 pints

2½ lbs. beef stew meat, cut into 1½-inch cubes

1½ tsp. vegetable oil

1 cup chopped onion (about 2 small)

½ cup garlic, minced fine

½ cup tomato paste

6 cups cubed and peeled potatoes (about 6 medium)

4 cups sliced carrots (about 8 small)

1¼ cups chopped celery (about 3 stalks)

2 tsp. salt

2 tsp. thyme

2 tsp. black pepper

water

1. Clean and prepare a pressure canner. Heat jars and lids in simmering water (do not boil). Keep them warm until ready to use. Set bands aside.

2. Heat oil in a 3-gallon pot. Dry the meat with a paper towel. Add meat to the hot oil to brown. Add onions and cook until caramelized and brown. Add the garlic. Cook another 3 minutes, being careful not to scorch the garlic. Add the tomato paste and cook until it cleans all the onion off the pot. Add remaining vegetables and seasonings to browned meat. Cover with boiling water. Bring stew to a boil. Remove from heat.

3. Scoop the hot stew into the prepared jars, leaving 1-inch headspace. Remove air bubbles and wipe the rim with a clean towel. Apply the lids and adjust the bands to fit tightly. Transfer the filled jars to pressure canner. Process at 10 pounds of pressure for 1 hour 15 minutes for pints and 1 hour 30 minutes for quarts, adjusting for altitude as needed. Start the timer when the pressure canner is up to temperature and pressure. When time is over, turn off the heat and allow the pressure cooker to decompress naturally. Do not run under water or remove the weight until the gauge reads "0" and the weight doesn't hiss when touched. That would be a sure sign that it needs more time to cool. Remove jars and cool in a draft-free area. Do not disturb them! Check lids for seal after 24 hours. Lid should not flex up and down when center is pressed. At this point, remove the rings. Wash and sanitize the outsides of the jars with warm soapy water.

I can't even imagine life growing up without chicken soup. It is so much a part of who I am, and when it comes to comfort food, it cannot be equaled. This is another fantastic recipe from Auntie Em.

chicken soup with soul

Yields 10 pints

3 medium onions, chopped

8 carrots, peeled and chopped

6 stalks celery, chopped

7 medium potatoes, peeled and chopped

water

garlic powder

black pepper

chicken bouillon (non-MSG variety, optional)

3 lbs. skinless, boneless chicken breasts, cooked

1. Mix onions, carrots, celery, and potatoes in a large plastic container. Cover with water until ready to use (this will prevent the potatoes from browning). Bring 12 cups of water to a boil. Prepare 10 pint jars for canning. In each jar place ⅛ teaspoon black ground pepper, ¼ teaspoon garlic powder, and 1 teaspoon chicken bouillon. Add ½ cup chopped chicken and 1 cup mixed veggies. Fill jar with water, leaving ½-inch headspace. Remove air bubbles, clean rims, and top with lids.

2. Place each jar in prepared pressure canner. Process at 10 pounds of pressure for 75 minutes, always adjusting for altitude as needed. Only start the timer when the pressure canner is up to temperature and pressure. When time is over, turn off the heat and allow the pressure cooker to decompress naturally. Do not run under water or remove the weight until the gauge reads "0" and the weight doesn't hiss when touched. That would be a sure sign that it needs more time to cool.

3. Remove jars and cool in a draft-free area. Do not disturb them! Check lids for seal after 24 hours. Lid should not flex up and down when center is pressed. At this point, remove the rings. Wash and sanitize the outsides of the jars with warm soapy water.

chili con carne asada

Yields 7 pints

5 lbs. lean ground beef

2 cups onion, chopped fine (about 2 medium)

2 cloves garlic, minced

8 cups tomatoes, peeled and diced

¼ cup chili powder

¼ cup ancho chile powder

2 Tbsp. salt

1 hot red pepper, minced

2 tsp. cumin seed, ground

2 tsp. coriander seed, ground

1 Tbsp. oregano, ground

1. Prepare pressure canner. Simmer jars and lids and set rings aside.

2. In a 2-gallon pot, brown beef and drain any extra fat. Add onions and garlic. Cook until clear. Add all remaining ingredients and simmer 25 minutes. Skim any excess fat before canning. Scoop beef mixture into canning jars, allowing 1-inch headspace. Purge any air bubbles. Top with canning lid and tighten ring to fingertip tight. Transfer jars to pressure canner. Process 1 hour 15 minutes. Only start the timer when the pressure canner is up to temperature and pressure.

3. When time is over, turn off the heat and allow the pressure cooker to decompress naturally. Do not run under water or remove the weight until the gauge reads "0" and the weight doesn't hiss when touched. That would be a sure sign that it needs more time to cool. Remove jars and cool in a draft-free area. Do not disturb them! Check lids for seal after 24 hours. Lid should not flex up and down when center is pressed. At this point, remove the rings. Wash and sanitize the outsides of the jars with warm soapy water.

4. To serve: Add cooked or canned pinto beans if desired and heat.

Money-saving tip: Ground turkey can be used instead of ground beef. It is usually much less per pound to purchase.

I love clam chowder, but we're landlocked in Arizona. I have to buy canned clams to make the soup base. It is well worth the effort to do, because this is a hearty and delicious soup to have any night of the week.

clammy clam chowder (base)

Yields 10 pints

8 oz. bacon, cooked and crumbled (fat drained off)

2 cups onion, minced

2 cups celery, diced

2 qts. clams, cleaned and chopped with juice

7 cups potatoes, peeled and diced

8 cups water

1 Tbsp. thyme

¼ cup garlic, minced

1 Tbsp. pepper

1 Tbsp. salt

1. In a 3-gallon pot, cook bacon until brown; drain excess fat. Add onions and celery and cook until tender. Add clams, potatoes, water, and seasoning. Get the pressure canner prepared. Heat jars and lids in simmering water, keeping ready for use (don't boil). Keep bands on hand. Pour into prepared jars, allowing 1-inch headspace. Purge jars of any air bubbles. Apply lids and rings, fingertip tight. Transfer jars to pressure canner. Process pints at 10 pounds of pressure for 1 hour 40 minutes, always adjusting for altitude as needed. Start the timer when the pressure canner is up to temperature and pressure.

2. When time is over, turn off the heat and allow the pressure cooker to decompress naturally. Do not run under water or remove the weight until the gauge reads "0" and the weight doesn't hiss when touched. That would be a sure sign that it needs more time to cool. Remove jars and cool in a draft-free area. Do not disturb them! Check lids for seal after 24 hours. Lid should not flex up and down when center is pressed. At this point, remove the rings. Wash and sanitize the outsides of the jars with warm soapy water.

③ This is the base for clam chowder. It is not recommended to add milk or butter before canning!

④ At service, add 2 tablespoons butter and 2 cups of milk to the base. Heat to serve. With the added milk, it will yield 1 quart of prepared soup.

Money-saving tip: Move somewhere where clams are cheap. Just kidding. I've used 8 cans of canned clams in this recipe, so I look diligently for deals at our local discount stores. If doing this, don't ever buy dented cans.

There's nothing more comforting than a familiar tomato soup. This is a smooth tomato with a kick of heat. Adjust the pepper to your liking.

spicy roasted tomato soup

Yields 4 pints

olive oil

4 cups onion, diced

2 cups celery, diced

2 cups red pepper, chopped

1 cup carrot, sliced thin

1 gallon tomatoes, peeled, chopped, and cored

¼ cup garlic, minced

1 tsp. clove, ground

1 Tbsp. red pepper flakes

1 cup brown sugar (optional)

1 Tbsp. salt

1 tsp. liquid smoke (optional)

① Heat a 3-gallon pot and add 1 tablespoon olive oil. Add the onions, celery, peppers, and carrots to the pot and let them sit unstirred for 5 minutes until they begin to caramelize. Add the tomatoes and all remaining ingredients. Simmer until all the vegetables are tender, about 20 minutes. Purée mixture in a blender 4–5 cups at a time until smooth. Transfer back to a large pot and simmer an additional 15 minutes. Get the pressure canner prepared. Heat jars and lids in simmering water, keeping ready for use (don't boil). Keep bands on hand.

② Pour into prepared jars, allowing 1-inch headspace. Purge jars of any air bubbles. Apply lids and rings, fingertip tight. Transfer jars to pressure canner. Process pints at 10 pounds of pressure for 20 minutes, always adjusting for altitude as needed. Start the timer when the pressure canner is up to temperature and pressure.

③ When time is over, turn off the heat and allow the pressure cooker to decompress naturally. Do not run under water or remove the weight until the gauge reads "0" and the weight doesn't hiss when touched. That would be a sure sign that it needs more time to cool. Remove jars and cool in a draft-free area. Do not disturb them! Check lids for seal after 24 hours. Lid should not flex up and down when center is pressed. At this point, remove the rings. Wash and sanitize the outsides of the jars with warm soapy water.

The very first time I ever remember visiting my dad at work for lunch was with a pot of homemade split pea soup in Mom's picnic basket. It was a thrill to see Daddy, but also exciting to share something from our house with him. Every single time I eat split pea soup, I think of him.

split pea and carrot soup

Yields 10 pints or 4 quarts

2 lbs. dry split peas

4 quarts water

3 cups carrots, sliced (about 6 medium)

2 cups onion, chopped

2 cups ham, cooked and diced

2 bay leaves

½ tsp. allspice

1 tsp. black pepper

1 tsp. thyme, ground

1 tsp. fennel seed, cracked

1. Combine all ingredients in a 2-gallon pot and simmer 1 hour until peas are soft. Meanwhile, prepare the pressure canner and jars, keeping jars and lids hot in simmering water. Pour the hot soup into jars, allowing 1-inch headspace. Purge of any air bubbles. Top with lids and hand-tighten rings. Transfer to a pressure canner. Process pints for 1 hour 15 minutes and quarts for 1 hour 30 minutes at 10 pounds of pressure. Always adjust as needed for altitude. Only start the timer when the pressure canner is up to temperature and pressure.

2. When time is over, turn off the heat and allow the pressure cooker to decompress naturally. Do not run under water or remove the weight until the gauge reads "0" and the weight doesn't hiss when touched. That would be a sure sign that it needs more time to cool. Remove jars and cool in a draft-free area. Do not disturb them! Check lids for seal after 24 hours. Lid should not flex up and down when center is pressed. At this point, remove the rings. Wash and sanitize the outsides of the jars with warm soapy water.

This beloved recipe was shared with me by my sister, Auntie Em, and it's one we keep for cold winter nights when we don't want to cook much but want to snuggle up with a hot bowl of comfort food. This is a keeper! It makes a lot of bottles as well. Awesome!

french ten-bean soup with ham

Yields 20 pints

3 lbs. ham, chopped

2 lbs. 10-bean soup mix

2 lbs. carrots, peeled and chopped

3 medium onions, chopped

4 stalks celery, chopped

5 small potatoes, chopped

¼ cup salt

¼ cup Herbes de Provence

water

1. Soak beans overnight (8–12 hours) and boil on stove for 30 minutes. Prepare 20 pint jars and rings. To each jar add ⅓ cup ham, ½ cup beans, ½ cup veggies, ½ teaspoon salt, ½ teaspoon dry Herbes de Provence, and 1 cup boiling water (up to 1-inch headspace). Fill jars and purge of air bubbles. Tighten the lids and rings and process in pressure canner 1 hour 15 minutes at 10 pounds pressure, adjusting as needed for altitude. Only start the timer when the pressure canner is up to temperature and pressure.

2. When time is over, turn off the heat and allow the pressure cooker to decompress naturally. Do not run under water or remove the weight until the gauge reads "0" and the weight doesn't hiss when touched. That would be a sure sign that it needs more time to cool. Remove jars and cool in a draft-free area. Do not disturb them! Check lids for seal after 24 hours. Lid should not flex up and down when center is pressed. At this point, remove the rings. Wash and sanitize the outsides of the jars with warm soapy water.

Homemade chicken stock without any artificial chemicals is well worth the effort to produce. Use it as the liquid for cooking rice and vegetables or as the base for a quick soup. The flavor is perfection.

basic chicken stock

Yields 4 quarts or 8 pints

4 lbs. chicken bones, cut into pieces (no skin or fat with little meat)

16 cups water

2 stalks celery, chopped

2 medium onions, quartered

1 Tbsp. salt

2 Tbsp. crushed peppercorn

2 bay leaves

1. In a 3-gallon stock pot, combine chicken and water. Bring to a boil. Reduce to a simmer and cook 2 hours. Add remaining ingredients and simmer 1 hour. Remove from heat. Skim off foam. Take out the chicken bones from stock and discard. Line a large sieve with cheesecloth and place over a large stock pot. Strain stock through a sieve or several layers of cheesecloth into the stock pot. Heat stock to a rolling boil. Get the pressure canner prepared. Heat jars and lids in simmering water, keeping ready for use (don't boil). Keep bands on hand.

2. Pour the hot chicken stock into hot jars, leaving 1-inch headspace. Wipe rim with a clean cloth, apply lids, and tighten rings. Transfer jars to a pressure canner and process at 10 pounds of pressure, 20 minutes for pints and 25 minutes for quarts, always adjusting as needed for altitude. Only start the timer when the pressure canner is up to temperature and pressure.

3. When time is over, turn off the heat and allow the pressure cooker to decompress naturally. Do not run under water or remove the weight until the gauge reads "0" and the weight doesn't hiss when touched. That would be a sure sign that it needs more time to cool. Remove jars and cool in a draft-free area. Do not disturb them! Check lids for seal after 24 hours. Lid should not flex up and down when center is pressed. At this point, remove the rings. Wash and sanitize the outsides of the jars with warm soapy water.

This beef stock is really deep in color and flavor, largely due to the fact that the bones are roasted in the oven with a little tomato paste before being slow-simmered for a few hours. It is an extra step that completely rounds out the flavor and boosts the depth of the stock. You'll never go back to boring stock again.

basic beef stock

Yields 8 pints or 4 quarts

4 lbs. meaty beef bones

½ cup tomato paste

16 cups water

2 medium onions, finely chopped

2 carrots, sliced

2 stalks celery, sliced

2 bay leaves

1 Tbsp. salt

1. Place beef bones in a large roaster and coat with tomato paste. Roast beef bones under broiler for 10–15 minutes until the tomato paste is very dark but not burned.

2. In a 3-gallon stock pot, combine the bones and water. Bring to a boil. Reduce to a simmer and cook 2 hours. Add remaining ingredients and simmer 1 hour. Remove from heat. Skim off foam.

3. Take out the beef bones from stock and discard. Line a large sieve with cheesecloth and place over a large stock pot. Strain stock through a sieve or several layers of cheesecloth into the stock pot. Heat stock to a rolling boil. Get the pressure canner prepared. Heat jars and lids in simmering water, keeping ready for use (don't boil). Keep bands on hand.

4. Pour the hot beef stock into hot jars, leaving 1-inch headspace. Wipe rim with a clean cloth, apply lids, and tighten rings. Transfer jars to a pressure canner and process at 10 pounds of pressure, 20 minutes for pints and 25 minutes for quarts, always adjusting as needed for altitude. Only start the timer when the pressure canner is up to temperature and pressure.

5. When time is over, turn off the heat and allow the pressure cooker to decompress naturally. Do not run under water or remove the weight until the gauge reads "0" and the weight doesn't hiss when touched. That would be a sure sign that it needs more time to cool. Remove jars and cool in a draft-free area. Do not disturb them! Check lids for seal after 24 hours. Lid should not flex up and down when center is pressed. At this point, remove the rings. Wash and sanitize the outsides of the jars with warm soapy water.

chapter six

sweet and specialty gourmet spreads and sauces

My kids were putting ketchup on everything and I didn't like all the added sugars and chemicals in most of the brands out there. I also didn't like the price of all the organic ketchups in the specialty stores! My recipe is a nice cross between my dear great-grandma's chile sauce and ketchup for dipping. This sauce is not to be confused with the high fructose corn syrup–laden, salty, one-dimensional sauce used in most American food. This has good depth and a lot of flavor. I think you'll be pleasantly pleased with the result. You may never go back to regular ketchup again!

best-ever gourmet homemade ketchup

yields 6–8 pints

2 #10 cans organic tomato purée (those are the big ones found at warehouse stores)

3 large onions, 1½-lb. puréed (in blender)

½ cup minced garlic, puréed (in blender)

1 tsp. cinnamon

1 Tbsp. black pepper

1 tsp. ground clove

1 tsp. ground allspice

2 tsp. ground celery seed

½ cup honey

1 cup apple cider vinegar

2 Tbsp. sea salt

2 Tbsp. smoked paprika

1 tsp. cayenne

1. In a 3-gallon pot, combine all ingredients and simmer over a very low heat for 2–3 hours until very thick. Purée and strain until desired consistency. Make ready your boiling water canner. Keep jars and lids in simmering water-bath on hand for when you are ready to use. Don't boil the lids. Set the separate lid-bands aside. Put in sterile jars. Seal the jars. Put in a boiling water-bath for 10 minutes. Remove from the water-bath and put on a clean towel. Do not disturb jars for 12 hours. This will ensure a good seal. Label and use within a year.

This recipe is a family favorite. It really is my great-grandma's chile sauce recipe and it is a tradition. I adjusted some of the spices, so I guess it is technically my recipe now. I use it in place of ketchup sometimes or as the base for BBQ sauce. It is also amazing in meatloaf and as a condiment for just about any meat. Once you try it, I think you will agree. It takes a good 2–3 hours of a low simmer to really achieve saucy perfection. Maybe someday I will have it in grocery stores. Until then, you will have to make your own. Enjoy.

grandma hill's chile sauce

yields 12 pints

6 qts. of tomato purée

2 large onions, chopped fine

4 red or green bell peppers, chopped fine

3 Tbsp. salt

2 cups brown sugar

1 Tbsp. curry paste

1½ tsp. clove, ground

1 Tbsp. nutmeg, ground

2 Tbsp. cayenne pepper

1½ tsp. allspice

2 Tbsp. cinnamon

1 Tbsp. celery seed

2 Tbsp. ground fennel seed

1½ cups cider vinegar

¼ cup garlic powder

1. Combine all ingredients in a very large 5-gallon stock pot and simmer 2–3 hours until very thick. Make ready your boiling water canner. Keep jars and lids in simmering water-bath on hand for when you are ready to use. Don't boil the lids. Set the separate lid-bands aside.

2. Spoon into sterile canning jars and seal with prepared canning lids. Boiling water process 20 minutes.

cry-to-mama hot sauce

Yields 6 half-pints

4 cups chopped hot red chili peppers or jalapeños
1½ cups golden raisins, rinsed
¼ cup chopped garlic
2 Tbsp. grated fresh ginger
2½ cups distilled vinegar
2½ cups granulated sugar
1 Tbsp. salt

① Make ready your boiling water canner. Keep jars and lids in simmering water-bath on hand for when you are ready to use. Don't boil the lids. Set the separate lid-bands aside.

② Purée peppers, raisins, garlic, and ginger in a blender with the vinegar until very smooth. Pour the vegetable mixture in a large stainless steel saucepan. Add the sugar and salt. Bring to a boil and cook 5–7 minutes.

③ Pour the hot sauce into hot jars, allowing ½-inch headspace. Remove air bubbles and remeasure headspace. If needed, add more sauce to meet recommended headspace. Wipe rim. Top jars with lids and bands. Transfer jars to a boiling water canner and process 10 minutes (adjusting for altitude). Remove from water and set to cool. Check the jars after 24 hours to be sure they have sealed.

Sometimes when I have a taco or burrito, I don't want chunky salsa, I just want hot sauce. This is a smooth, delicious taco sauce. If you want it to be spicy, use cayenne pepper in place of part of the chili powder.

red rage taco sauce

yields 6 half-pints

5 cups water

3 cups tomato paste (about 2 (12-oz.) cans)

½ cup cider vinegar

½ cup bottled lemon juice (5% acidity)

½ cup corn syrup

2 Tbsp. chili powder

1 Tbsp. fresh ground Ancho chile

1 Tbsp. salt

1 tsp. ground cumin

1 tsp. cayenne pepper

1. Make ready your boiling water canner. Keep jars and lids in simmering water-bath on hand for when you are ready to use. Don't boil the lids. Set the separate lid-bands aside.

2. In a large stainless steel pot, combine all ingredients and bring to a boil. Reduce heat and simmer 35 minutes until the mixture is the consistency of a thin barbecue sauce. Pour the hot sauce into hot jars, allowing ½-inch headspace. Remove air bubbles. Wipe rim. Apply lid and tighten band until fit is fingertip tight. Transfer jars to a boiling water canner for 30 minutes, adjusting for altitude. Remove jars and cool.

This is my secret recipe, though after this book comes out, it won't be secret anymore. It is perfect for ribs and chicken or anywhere you would use barbecue sauce. It is genius sauce.

sweet-baby-genius barbecue sauce

Yields 4–6 pints (depending on the thickness of the sauce)

20 cups tomato purée (about 21 medium, peeled and puréed)

1½ cups onion, finely minced (about 3 medium)

½ cup garlic, finely minced

1½ cups lightly packed brown sugar

½ cup molasses

1 cup cider vinegar (5% acidity)

½ cup lemon juice

1 Tbsp. hot pepper flakes

1 Tbsp. fresh ground black pepper

1 Tbsp. celery seeds

2 Tbsp. salt

2 Tbsp. dry mustard

1 tsp. ground cumin

1 tsp. ground coriander seed

1 tsp. liquid smoke (optional)

1. Make ready your boiling water canner. Keep jars and lids in simmering water-bath on hand for when you are ready to use. Don't boil the lids. Set the separate lid-bands aside.

2. In a 2-gallon stainless steel saucepan, combine all ingredients and simmer 30–35 minutes until the consistency of a thin barbecue sauce.

3. Pour hot sauce into hot sterile jars, allowing ½-inch headspace. Be sure to remove any air bubbles. Wipe the rim of the jar with a clean cloth. Top with lid and tighten ring fingertip tight. Transfer jars to a boiling water canner and process 20 minutes, adjusting for altitude. Remove from water and allow to cool completely 12–24 hours. Check seals.

angry georgia peach barbecue sauce

Yields 8 half-pint jars

8 cups peaches, pitted and peeled (about 4 lbs. or 11 medium)

1 cup yellow or red jalapeño pepper, finely chopped, seeded (about 1 large)

½ cup onion, chopped (about 1 large)

⅓ cup garlic, finely chopped (about 28 cloves)

1¼ cups honey

¾ cup cider vinegar

2 tsp. hot pepper flakes

1 Tbsp. dry mustard

2 tsp. salt

⅛ tsp. liquid smoke flavor

1. Make ready your boiling water canner. Keep jars and lids in simmering water-bath on hand for when you are ready to use. Don't boil the lids. Set the separate lid-bands aside.

2. Put all ingredients in a large blender or work in batches. Purée until a smooth consistency. Pour the puréed mixture in a large gallon-sized saucepan and simmer 25–30 minutes.

3. Pour hot sauce into hot sterile jars, allowing ½-inch headspace. Be sure to remove any air bubbles. Wipe the rim of the jar with a clean cloth. Top with lid and tighten ring fingertip tight. Transfer jars to a boiling water canner and process 15 minutes, adjusting for altitude. Remove from water and allow to cool completely 12–24 hours. Check seals.

I came up with this recipe many years ago when I first started working with a local organic tomato farmer. I was paid in tomatoes most of the time, and that was a good thing! It felt like I was getting salsa for free! I am not kidding when I say that my husband would literally drink bottles of this homemade salsa. It is still a go-to family favorite!

chef's best roasted tomato fajita salsa

Yields 6 pints

1 Tbsp. olive oil

1 cup onions, diced (1 medium)

¼ cup garlic, minced

6 lbs. tomatoes, blanched and peeled, half puréed, half rough-chopped (12 cups total)

½ cup Hatch green chiles, roasted, peeled and seeded

¼ cup Frank's® RedHot Sauce

1 cup apple cider vinegar

1 Tbsp. cumin, ground

1 Tbsp. oregano, dry

1 Tbsp. black pepper, fresh cracked

2 tsp. coriander seed, ground

1 Tbsp. salt

3 Tbsp. cilantro, chopped

½ tsp. liquid smoke (optional)

1. Make ready your boiling water canner. Keep jars and lids in simmering water-bath on hand for when you are ready to use. Don't boil the lids. Set the separate lid-bands aside.

2. In a heavy 2-gallon stock pot, heat olive oil until almost smoking. Put onions in pan. Do not stir for 5 minutes until one side of the onions are very dark brown (as you would for fajitas). Add the garlic and cook 2–3 minutes. Add all remaining ingredients. Simmer 20 minutes uncovered until thickened. Place salsa in sterile canning jars with ½-inch head space. Process 15 minutes for pints and 20 minutes for quart jars.

Right next to the red salsa on the table, we always have to have the green stuff. Tomatillos can be found in most Mexican food sections of grocery stores across the southwestern United States and are available fresh during the summer months. They look like green tomatoes with a paper-like pod coating the fruit. Tomatillos make a sauce that is sweet and tangy. I use a little sweetener in mine because we adore it with the addition of a kiss of sweetness. Use the full amount of cilantro as well; it will really kick up the flavor. Drizzle it over your burritos. It is incredible. I have to hide it from my family if I want any for myself!

our famous green tomatillo salsa

Yields 6 pints

11 cups chopped, cored, and husked tomatillos

2 cups onion, chopped

1 cup minced serrano green chili peppers

12 cloves garlic, minced

1 bunch cilantro, minced

2 tsp. cumin, ground

1 Tbsp. plus 1 tsp. salt

1 Tbsp. oregano, dried

2 cups vinegar (5% acidity or higher)

½ cup fresh lime juice

1 cup sugar

1. Prepare your boiling water canner. Keep jars and lids in a simmering water-bath until you are ready to use. Don't boil the lids. Set the separate lid-bands aside.

2. Purée the tomatillos and onions in a blender until smooth. Combine all ingredients in a large sauce pot. Bring mixture to a boil. Reduce heat and simmer for 10 minutes. Ladle hot salsa into hot jars, leaving a ¼-inch headspace. Adjust two-piece caps. Process 15 minutes in a boiling water canner. Remove from canner and place on dry kitchen towel. Allow to cool for 12 hours. Check the seals. If properly sealed, store for up to a year. If it didn't seal, it may be refrigerated up to 2 months.

pineapple pepper salsa

Yields 8 half-pints

6 cups chopped fresh pineapple

6 jalapeños, minced

1 onion, peeled and chopped

6 garlic cloves, minced

2 tsp. oregano, ground

2 tsp. coriander, ground

1 tsp. cumin, ground

1 Tbsp. salt

1 cup apple cider vinegar

½ cup cilantro, minced

1. Make ready your boiling water canner. Keep jars and lids in simmering water-bath on hand for when you are ready to use. Don't boil the lids. Set the separate lid-bands aside.

2. Place all ingredients except the cilantro in a 5–6 quart heavy pot and boil over medium-high heat about 5 minutes, then reduce to a simmer and cook 10–15 minutes more. Add cilantro. Ladle your hot salsa into prepared jars with a sterile cup, leaving ¼-inch head space. Wipe the jar rims. Seal the jars with the two-piece caps, hand-tightening the bands.

3. Process the filled jars in a water-bath for 10 minutes from the point of boiling. Remove the jars from the boiling water with a jar lifter. Place them on a clean kitchen towel or paper towels away from drafts. After the jars cool completely (I leave undisturbed for 12 hours), test the seals. If you find jars that haven't sealed, refrigerate them and use them within 2 months.

hot jalapeño salsa

Yields 6 pints

4 lbs. tomatoes, peeled and chopped to measure 3 cups

1 lb. diced jalapeño chiles, roasted with the peels, seeds, and stems removed

1 cup onion, minced (about 1 medium)

6 cloves garlic, minced

¼ cup cilantro, freshly minced

1 Tbsp. oregano, dry

1½ tsp. kosher salt

1½ tsp. cumin, ground

1 cup apple cider vinegar

1. Make ready your boiling water canner. Keep jars and lids in simmering water-bath on hand for when you are ready to use. Don't boil the lids. Set the separate lid-bands aside. Place all the ingredients in a 5- to 6-quart pot. Bring all ingredients to a boil over high heat, stirring to combine. Reduce the heat to low and simmer uncovered for 10 minutes.

2. Ladle your hot salsa into the prepared jars, leaving headspace of ¼ inch. Wipe the jar rims; seal the jars with two-piece caps, hand-tightening the bands. Process the filled jars in a water boiling water-bath for 10 minutes from the point of boiling.

3. Remove the jars from the boiling water with a jar lifter. Place them on a clean kitchen towel or paper towels away from any draft. After the jars cool, test the seals. If you find jars that haven't sealed, refrigerate them and use them within 2 months.

The first time I heard about the combination of cucumber and pepper in salsa, I was intrigued. It sounded light and fresh. I was not disappointed. This is a wonderful salsa for seafood and hot summer nights.

cucumber banana pepper salsa

Yields 8 half-pint jars

8 cups tomatoes, peeled and diced

½ cup banana pepper, minced (about 3)*

½ cup onion, peeled and chopped

1 cup cucumber, peeled and chopped

6 garlic cloves, minced

2 tsp. ground oregano

2 tsp. ground coriander

1 tsp. ground cumin

1 Tbsp. salt

1 cup apple cider vinegar

½ cup minced cilantro

1. Make ready your boiling water canner. Keep jars and lids in simmering water-bath on hand for when you are ready to use. Don't boil the lids. Set the separate lid-bands aside.

2. Place all ingredients except the cilantro in a 5–6 quart heavy pot and boil over medium-high heat about 5 minutes. Reduce to a simmer and cook 10–15 minutes more. Add cilantro. Ladle your hot salsa into prepared jars with a sterile cup, leaving ¼-inch headspace. Wipe the jar rims. Seal the jars with the two-piece caps, hand tightening the bands. Process the filled jars in a water-bath for 10 minutes from the point of boiling. Remove the jars from the boiling water with a jar lifter. Place them on a clean kitchen towel or paper towels away from drafts. After the jars cool completely (I leave undisturbed for 12 hours), test the seals. If you find jars that haven't sealed, refrigerate them and use them within 2 months.

*A banana-shaped pepper that changes from pale to deep yellow or orange as they mature. These are easily confused with hotter yellow wax peppers. Sample before using.

This delicate dessert syrup is ideal for crêpes, drizzled over fruit, or poured over ice cream. I love it on waffles.

apple pecan syrup

Yields 4 half-pints

1 cup peeled and diced green apples

1½ cups dark corn syrup (non-GMO)

1 cup pure maple syrup

½ cup water

½ cup granulated sugar

2 tsp. double-strength pure vanilla

2 cups pecans, chopped

1. Make ready your boiling water canner. Keep jars and lids in simmering water-bath on hand for when you are ready to use. Don't boil the lids. Set the separate lid-bands aside. In a large stainless steel saucepan, combine all ingredients except the nuts and simmer on low for 15 minutes.

2. Add the nuts and cook 5 minutes more. Pour the hot syrup into hot jars, allowing ¼-inch headspace. Wipe the rim with a clean cloth and seal lids finger tight. Transfer to a boiling water-bath canner and process 10 minutes, always adjusting as necessary for altitude. Remove jars from the water and cool on a clean towel or rack away from drafts. Check lids after 24 hours to ensure they are sealed correctly.

Money-saving tip: Purchase the nuts in bulk whenever possible to cut the cost of this sauce. You can use less nuts, but the flavor will not be warm or well rounded.

chunky peach melba sauce

Yields 7 half pints

6 cups peaches, peeled, pitted, and chopped

2 cups lightly packed brown sugar

2 cups granulated sugar

1 cup puréed raspberries

¼ tsp. natural lemon oil*

1 tsp. natural orange brandy-flavored oil

1. Make ready your boiling water canner. Keep jars and lids in simmering water-bath on hand for when you are ready to use. Don't boil the lids. Set the separate lid-bands aside. In a large stainless steel pot, combine the peaches, brown sugar, granulated sugar, raspberry purée, and flavor oils. Bring to a boil over high heat, stirring constantly, until sugar dissolves. Reduce heat and boil gently, stirring occasionally, until thickened, about 10 minutes.

2. Pour the hot syrup into the hot prepared jars, allowing ¼-inch headspace. Wipe the rims with a clean cloth. Top with lids. Tighten bands to fingertip tight. Transfer jars to a boiling water-bath canner and process 10 minutes, always adjusting as needed for altitude. Remove jars from the water and place on a clean dry cloth. Allow to cool. Check seal after 24 hours.

*Lemon oil is a natural extract of lemon peel found in health-food stores.

Money-saving tip: When I make this sauce in the off season for peaches, the cost of frozen peaches is almost always lower than the fresh fruit. In that case, I will defrost the bag, chop the fruit, and proceed with the recipe.

blueberry lemon syrup

Yields 3 pints

8 cups blueberries, crushed (about 3½ lbs.)

3 cups granulated sugar

2 Tbsp. lemon juice

½ tsp. lemon oil*

1 tsp. Bavarian cream LorAnn® natural flavoring oil

1. Make ready your boiling water canner. Keep jars and lids in simmering water-bath on hand for when you are ready to use. Don't boil the lids. Set the separate lid-bands aside.

2. Puree berries in a blender until smooth. Transfer to a half-gallon stainless steel pot and add remaining ingredients. Boil 10 minutes until sugar is dissolved and the sauce is slightly thick, but not jam. Pour the hot syrup into the hot prepared jars, allowing ¼-inch headspace. Wipe the rims with a clean cloth. Top with lids.

3. Tighten bands to fingertip tight. Transfer jars to a boiling water-bath canner and process 10 minutes, always adjusting as needed for altitude. Remove jars from the water and place on a clean, dry cloth. Allow to cool. Check seal after 24 hours.

*Lemon oil is a natural extract of lemon peel found in health-food stores.

Money-saving tip: Purchase berries when they are at the peak of freshness when making this sauce. When they are not in season and you still want to cut the cost, they can be purchased frozen and allowed to defrost before making the sauce.

blackberry lime sauce

Yields 3 pints or 6 half-pints

8 cups blackberries, crushed (about 3½ lbs.)
3 cups granulated sugar
2 Tbsp. lime juice
½ tsp. LorAnn® natural lime oil*

1. Make ready your boiling water canner. Keep jars and lids in simmering water-bath on hand for when you are ready to use. Don't boil the lids. Set the separate lid-bands aside.

2. Puree berries in a blender until smooth. Transfer to a large half-gallon stainless steel pot and add remaining ingredients. Boil 10 minutes until sugar is dissolved and the sauce is slightly thick but not jam. Pour the hot syrup into the hot prepared jars, allowing ¼-inch headspace. Wipe the rims with a clean cloth. Top with lids. Tighten bands to fingertip tight.

3. Transfer jars to a boiling water-bath canner and process 10 minutes, always adjusting as needed for altitude. Remove jars from the water and place on a clean, dry cloth. Allow to cool. Check seal after 24 hours.

*This is a natural lime oil sold in cake-decorating sections of craft stores and online at LorAnn.com.

cooking measurement equivalents

Cups	Tablespoons	Fluid Ounces
⅛ cup	2 Tbsp.	1 fl. oz.
¼ cup	4 Tbsp.	2 fl. oz.
⅓ cup	5 Tbsp. + 1 tsp.	
½ cup	8 Tbsp.	4 fl. oz.
⅔ cup	10 Tbsp. + 2 tsp.	
¾ cup	12 Tbsp.	6 fl. oz.
1 cup	16 Tbsp.	8 fl. oz.

Cups	Fluid Ounces	Pints/Quarts/Gallons
1 cup	8 fl. oz.	½ pint
2 cups	16 fl. oz.	1 pint = ½ quart
3 cups	24 fl. oz.	1½ pints
4 cups	32 fl. oz.	2 pints = 1 quart
8 cups	64 fl. oz.	2 quarts = ½ gallon
16 cups	128 fl. oz.	4 quarts = 1 gallon

Other Helpful Equivalents

1 Tbsp.	3 tsp.
8 oz.	½ lb.
16 oz.	1 lb.

metric measurement equivalents

Approximate Weight Equivalents

Ounces	Pounds	Grams
4 oz.	¼ lb.	113 g
5 oz.		142 g
6 oz.		170 g
8 oz.	½ lb.	227 g
9 oz.		255 g
12 oz.	¾ lb.	340 g
16 oz.	1 lb.	454 g

Approximate Volume Equivalents

Cups	US Fluid Ounces	Milliliters
⅛ cup	1 fl. oz.	30 ml
¼ cup	2 fl. oz.	59 ml
½ cup	4 fl. oz.	118 ml
¾ cup	6 fl. oz.	177 ml
1 cup	8 fl. oz.	237 ml

Other Helpful Equivalents

½ tsp.	2½ ml
1 tsp.	5 ml
1 Tbsp.	15 ml

Index

about the author

Chef Stephanie Petersen is a classically trained chef, cooking instructor, and cookbook author, as well as a dynamic television and radio personality. Stephanie has been a large group and personal cooking instructor since 2004 and continues to be heavily involved with culinary education around the country. She is the corporate chef for one of the largest grain companies on the west coast, Honeyville Food Products. She is, in every way, a real down-to-earth gal who adores teaching, laughing, loving, and connecting with new people every day. Stephanie lives in Phoenix, Arizona, with her husband and two children.